Pay Attention!

Pay Attention!

How to Get, Keep, and Use Attention to Grow Your Business

Cassandra M. Bailey and Dana M. Schmidt

BUSINESS EXPERT PRESS

Leader in applied, concise business books

Pay Attention!:
How to Get, Keep, and Use Attention to Grow Your Business

First published in 2022 by
Business Expert Press, LLC
222 East 46th Street, New York, NY 10017
www.businessexpertpress.com

ISBN-13: 978-1-63742-264-9 (paperback)
ISBN-13: 978-1-63742-265-6 (e-book)

Business Expert Press Business Career Development Collection

First edition: 2022

10 9 8 7 6 5 4 3 2 1

Description

Getting, keeping, and using attention is one of the hardest and most important challenges for marketers today. People's attention is being pulled in a million different directions by social media, podcasts, TV, Facebook/Instagram, family, friends, politics, the list goes on.

Marketing veterans Cassandra Bailey and Dana Schmidt have developed a simple model that any business or nonprofit can use to identify which types of attention they need and create plans to go get them. In a step-by-step process, the authors outline the five types of attention, six potential audiences, three parts of messaging, five kinds of content, four bridges to move people, and a surround sound approach to pull it all together.

The result is the one thing all brands need today: **Sustained attention from the people who matter most.**

Keywords

marketing; communications; strategy; messaging; promotion; public relations; social media; e-mail marketing; advertising

Contents

Testimonials

"In a world where marketing strategies are endless, Cass and Dana explore a simple yet innovative process on how to ensure sustained attention to your brand. I encourage business owners to provide copies of this book to their marketing teams so they can watch how their mindset and strategies evolve—you won't be disappointed."—**Ami Kassar, Cofounder and CEO of Multifunding; Author of** *The Growth Dilemma: Determining Your Entrepreneurial Type to Find Your Financing Comfort Zone*

"Just like people, organizations need attention to survive and thrive. And just how people of different personalities crave different forms of attention, organizations have different needs as well. In this groundbreaking book, Cassandra Bailey and Dana Schmidt will show you how to get attention and keep it. Pay Attention! *will change the way you go about creating brand and organizational awareness."*—**Merrick Rosenberg, CEO of Take Flight Learning and author of** *The Chameleon and Which Bird Are You?*

"Like many industries, marketing has undergone a tremendous digital transformation. Cass and Dana understand all the choices that businesses can make and the complexities these choices bring. Their explanations, case studies, and exercises help cut through these challenges to make today's marketing understandable and actionable."—**Tracey Welson-Rossman, Chief Marketing Officer, Chariot Solutions; Founder, TechGirlz.org**

Acknowledgments

We've both dreamt of writing a book for a long time, albeit separately. It finally came together over the course of a year as we worked remotely due to COVID-19. Even though we were not physically in the same place, we managed to pull all our thoughts, insights, and experiences together thanks to the help and support of many talented people.

Leo Manning was critical to the creation of the Attention Model. It honestly would not exist without him. He and Dana completed the initial work identifying the four, and then five, types of attention. Leo saw the graphical articulation of the whole model in his head and then turned it into something anyone could explain. This model became the backbone of the presentation Cass gave that got the interest of an editor. That interest became this book. Leo is also the visionary designer of the cover of this book, which brings us so much joy.

We also must thank our editor, Vilma Barr, and the whole team at Business Expert Press. When she and Cass had lunch in October 2020, we did not believe it was possible for us to write a book. But Vilma read some of Cass' blogs, eBooks, and white papers, and told us that we had already written a book—just a book in pieces. Her encouragement, guidance, and support throughout this process, even during some writing delays, have been invaluable.

Our team at Slice Communications, our agency, has been the foundation on which the Attention Model and this book were formed. Dea Maddox Tuwalski has been our rock, our proofreader, our coach, our translator, and the remover of all barriers. Rayce Rollins has been our cheerleader, and his unbridled excitement when we showed him the model for the first time convinced us we had something that might really help people. During the course of writing this book, three individuals joined our team as we were struggling to get the book done. Kija Chronister put a marketing plan in place for the book and helped to manage the editing process. Charlotte Bausch and Mary McCusker came on board and immediately used their copyediting and writing experience to dot every "I" and cross every "T." To Dea, Kija, Charlotte, and Mary—our Book Committee team who drove this book over the finish line—thank you for your many hours of reading, editing, collaboration, and support; you have all been very invaluable throughout this process. Sara McGovern, Marissa Bruette, Andrew Shober, Grace Andrake, Caroline Hromy, Mark Ladley, Aleah Conlin, Matt Smith, Adrian Heredia, Tiffany Coppola, and our whole Slice Fam have pushed and challenged us along the way. They have been the guinea pigs, testers, and champions for the model, showing us where we needed to make improvements and highlighting what really worked.

As an agency, our clients are our shareholders. We are so thankful for each and every one of them who believe in the attention-based approach and practice it every day. Many of them have been with us for years and have provided the insights necessary to develop our approach. They challenge and support us as we grow in our marketing expertise and business knowledge. We want to especially thank those whose stories we reference anonymously throughout the book.

We are both so thankful for our mentors who have given us advice and truth throughout our careers. Cass needs to thank Chris Schalleur, Alex Ankudovich, Eric Griffin, Chad Moore, Jason Johnson, and Brad Wolfe, who always have her back. She also needs to acknowledge Harry Haber for all his good advice and tough challenges over the years. Dana is incredibly appreciative of the amazing listeners and leaders who have inspired her along the way, like Paula Butler, Cara Schneider, Tony Sadowski, and Danny Gardner—and special thanks to John Freeman, who reminded her to just keep writing.

There were two additional women who really helped move this project forward and get it done. Without them, it would have just been a collection of loosely related words and thoughts in a Google Doc somewhere. Laura Berry helped craft the narrative and structure and Maia Nikitina turned the manuscript into something readable. Thank you both. Your fingerprints and hearts are all over the pages.

As working moms, and now authors, we juggle a lot. Our families are the centers of our lives, and they make it all worth it. Caia, Cooper, Mia, Alexandra, and Camden, you are everything to us. You are the sun, the moon, the stars, and the waves. We love you forever and always.

A few years ago, Chris Snyder changed Cass' life. He showed her that she was capable of great things. He believed in her, told her she was good at what she does, and celebrated her successes with her. He held her when she cried and picked her up when she fell. Cass never could have written this book without him. Chris, you are the pinnacle.

For Dana, Jesse McKevitt has always brought out the "est" in her. The bravest, the boldest, and on occasion, the silliest. For 10 years and counting, his encouragement has made even the most impossible tasks feel manageable. Jesse, your partnership in this life is the greatest gift of all, and Dana can't thank you enough for the support and motivation—and for always saving her the last piece of cheese.

We are both very lucky to have wonderful, supportive parents. Cheryl, Rob, Nancy, and Karl understand that we are creative, ambitious, and driven women who stand on their shoulders. Their love and guidance have been the bedrock of our successes.

There are many more people to thank, we are sure. We appreciate each and every one of them, though they are unnamed here. We also appreciate you! Thank you for taking the time to explore a new way to think about your marketing communications efforts. Thank you for giving this approach a chance. And thank you for giving us the opportunity to be your guides on this journey.

Introduction

Getting, Keeping, and Using Attention

Attention is the scarcest resource in the modern world today. People had very little of it before the 2020 COVID-19 pandemic and now they have even less. Our attention is pulled in a million different directions in a day, sometimes literally, as we are subject to messages, images, and information from thousands of different sources across our laptops, TVs, and mobile phones. Most American adults use Facebook. They're on it multiple times a day and they see thousands of posts every time they scroll. Most American teens watch hundreds of hours of YouTube every year. The algorithms are designed to keep them on the website, watching videos from paid and unpaid creators and getting ads fed to them every few minutes. Meanwhile, they also have the TV on in the background and are checking their e-mail on their phone or laptop. Attention is being paid to everything and nothing all at the same time.

For many years now, we have been working in the attention business. Some call it marketing. Others call it advertising or public relations (PR) or social media. But no matter what you call it, it is about getting, keeping, and using attention. Attention is at the center of everything. If people do not know you exist, they cannot do business with you, buy from you, or tell others to buy from you. It's simply impossible.

Our company, Slice Communications, gets people to pay attention! We're the experts in harnessing the power of "surround sound" communication to turn awareness into advocacy via our proprietary *Five Types of Attention*. For the last 12 years, our strategic focus on attention has helped our clients achieve and surpass their business goals.

In this book, we are going to explore what attention is and how to get it for your business. We'll explore the five types of attention, what they are, what they mean, and in what order you need to get them. Attention is not valuable in and of itself. Instead, it must come from the right people. For that reason, we will outline the six audiences that are the most important to most businesses.

Many business owners and marketers get stuck when it comes to what they say to people to get their attention. That is because they are usually too focused on what they want to communicate and not on what their audiences want or need to hear. A few chapters will be dedicated to thinking about messaging in new and different ways that lead to compelling content—something that gets people to take the actions you need to grow your business.

In our many years of working with middle market businesses, nonprofits, startups, and Fortune 500 companies, we have seen over and over again that marketing communications plans fail when there is no alignment in the internal team. For that reason, we have included a chapter on how to get and maintain a shared vision, priorities, and definition of success. Of course, this is something that needs to be done regularly, so we have included a process that anyone can follow.

People's attention is always shifting, which means that how you market to them must change as well. The best way to do this is to accept that learning, changing, and improving are and always will be part of marketing. No good marketing strategy is the same year after year. Instead, we recommend that you collect data and information that informs the changes that need to be made weekly and that you revisit the plan quarterly. In the middle of the book, there are some samples of how to do this so your whole organization can focus on what really matters and stop just "doing marketing."

Throughout the book, we will share stories of companies who have gotten the attention of the right people at the right time to move the needle for their organizations. Our hope is that these stories take the fear out of trying something new with your marketing communications in the coming year. When you see the creative risk taking that other companies have enjoyed, you may also be willing to abandon what you have been doing for years in favor of something that takes into account the new reality of marketing to people who do not give up their attention easily.

There is an unfortunate perception that marketing is easy, that anyone can do it. Quite often, this critical business function is given to someone who has no training or background in it because they seem to communicate well. We bring this up for two reasons. If you are a business owner in a medium or small company, please ensure the people you have tasked with marketing your company are well-resourced. They need professional development and mentors. They cannot get the attention your organization critically needs if their work is considered "nice to have" or an afterthought. Investing in marketing is investing in your business.

If you are a marketing professional reading this book, use it as an opportunity to ask for what you need. Lay out the challenges to getting attention, ensure your internal team is aligned, set a clear vision for your success, make your work a priority, and do not settle for being the last item on the agenda. What you do can make or break a company, even if your boss doesn't understand that. Embrace your power and use it.

Our hope for you is simple: That after you finish reading this book, you do one thing that increases the attention you are getting. That increase can mean more sales, a better reputation, more employee applications, or the opportunity to sell the company. Take it seriously, invest in it, and you will see the difference in your bottom line.

PART I

Strategy

CHAPTER 1

The Five Types of Attention

Understanding Why Attention Is the Key to Your Business Success

Not all attention is created equal. It can be very different, depending on your targeted audience, what they want, and how they get news and information. For that reason, we, in conjunction with our team, have defined five types of attention (see Figure 1.1) that all organizations need in order to grow. All marketing personnel need to carefully understand what they have and what they need before determining what to do with their marketing.

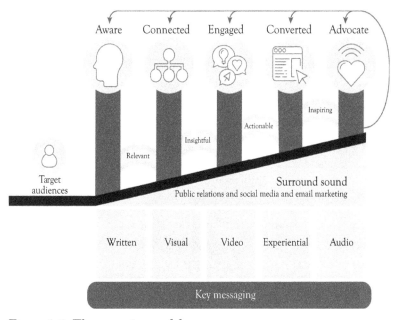

Figure 1.1 The attention model

Before we get into the types of attention, we should be honest with ourselves about how our customers buy, and how we buy, too. Very rarely do we see something and buy it in that instance. Sure, it happens. It just does not happen often and it almost never happens in business-to-business (B2B) transactions. Even when you are standing in line at the grocery store and pick up a pack of gum, you will likely make the decision on which pack of gum to buy based on your past experience, what you know about the different brands, and what you saw most recently in an advertisement.

In 1898, Elias St. Elmo Lewis came up with the idea of the sales funnel, which is also called the marketing funnel. He believed that people who were making decisions about what to buy experienced four phases: awareness, interest, desire, and action (Strong 1925, 9). Many executives still believe that is how things work. We, and many others who study purchasing behavior, disagree. In the 19th century, there were not many choices or sources of information. Most grocers offered one type of milk, maybe two. In the 21st century, things are completely different. Just go into the milk aisle today, and you will see what we mean. There are so many different kinds of milk, and most of them don't even come from cows, much to the dairy industry's dismay. Now imagine a world where everyone got their news from a small handful of newspapers. There simply wasn't as much information as we have now, and things moved very slowly. There were not even that many opportunities to advertise. Public relations did not exist. Compare that to today, when we get news from a variety of sources, every second of every day.

We subscribe to those who believe the sales and marketing process is not a straight line—it is pretzel-shaped (see Figure 1.2). The fact that we are based in Philadelphia, a city famous for its pretzels, is not the only reason we believe this. We buy this way, and so do most others. The process starts at awareness, just as Elias St. Elmo Lewis suggested. But from there, the road is winding. People hear about you, they check out your website, they see some ads from you on their LinkedIn or Facebook accounts, they sign up for a special offer you are marketing, they check out your website again, they look at reviews or ask other people about you, they run into your brand at an event, they sign up for a coupon or webinar or white paper, they go to your website again, they get an e-mail from you, and they finally decide to make a purchase or get a quote. Doesn't this feel much more authentic than a direct, four-step purchasing journey?

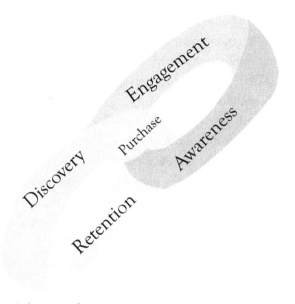

Figure 1.2 Sales pretzel

As an aside, Elias St. Elmo Lewis was also a Philadelphian and we believe, if he were still alive today, he would also advocate for a pretzel-shaped sales and marketing journey.

According to a study of B2B marketing conducted by Google and Millward Brown Digital, B2B buyers have already completed 12 research steps, including having searched for comparison products, watched videos, and read reviews, before contemplating contacting businesses directly (Snyder and Hilal 2015). They can move themselves through the buying journey as long as the content they are looking for is available and there are multiple ways to connect and engage with the company from which they will eventually buy. That is why understanding and planning for the five types of attention should be the cornerstone of any marketing strategy.

Awareness

Awareness is the first and most important form of attention. Without it, nothing else happens. If people don't know you exist, they can't do business with you. However, many businesses don't start their market-ing here. They try to skip directly to using marketing to generate leads or close deals. This is a mistake. Marketing is not sales. Yes, it can and should support sales. They should work together. And there are certain types of direct response marketing that can generate leads once all the other types of attention are earned. But the fundamental truth is that thinking your marketing can skip right to converted attention is foolish; it sets the marketing team or agency up for failure and it creates stress within your organization.

So let's start at the very beginning: What is awareness? Awareness is nothing more than a thought. An impression is made on a brain. An idea is formed about the company, the product, the service, or the concept. In the marketing realm, it typically starts when someone sees or hears something. Most new impressions happen online today, though they can also occur in the car via a billboard, on the radio or a podcast, or in-person at a store or trade show.

So how do you get in front of people who do not know you exist? Getting covered in the news is often the broadest and most widespread way to get awareness. Traditional advertising—newspaper ads, billboards, TV commercials, and so on—are another way. News coverage has the upside of being highly credible because people understand that a journalist and an editor chose to do a story about you, while they know that advertising is self-promotion. On the other hand, advertising has the benefit of being controllable and certain. Businesses can determine when an ad appears, where it appears, and what it says. Media coverage provides none of that.

Digital marketing and advertising offer new and different ways to create brand awareness. Social media ads let marketers send messages to people who live in New Jersey, have grandchildren, own a dog, fly on Southwest, drink Coors Light, and are thinking about buying a new car. Messages and ads can be sent directly to them on Facebook, Instagram, and their entire ad network to create awareness. Marketers can know exactly how many times people see those ads, what percentage of the audience interacts with them, and what percentage of the audience acts on them. The same is true for LinkedIn, Twitter, Pinterest, and YouTube. The potential to create awareness with people who are in a targeted demographic or who have preferred psychographics is limitless. We will talk more about psychographics in another chapter, but understanding them is often the work that unlocks truly compelling content.

The really challenging part of awareness is that it can be lost at any time. Many brands and messages are simply forgettable. Our goal used to be to create seven impressions with a targeted audience in order to create awareness. Now, thanks to an increase in media and competition, that number is somewhere between 11 and 13. Most companies don't realize that, and their marketing plans don't account for the related expense of creating so many impressions before getting to awareness.

The other mistake many businesses make is that they give up on brand awareness after a predesignated timeframe. Smart brands, including many of those you buy, never give up. They just keep working on awareness over and over again. They recognize that buyers change, new buyers are born or enter the market every day, old buyers leave or die. It is a moving target that requires constant investment.

Similarly, the competitive landscape is always changing and new players are constantly trying to get people to pay attention to them and forget you. Recently on a podcast, the host was talking about a new brand of sheets. He went on and on about how comfortable they were, that he had them in his house, and how they made his bed his happy place. While listening, we realized that this same host, in a previous year, also talked about a totally different brand of sheets that had done all the same things for him. Last year's brand was largely forgotten for us, and it sounded like for him too.

Many years ago, we worked with an electric company that was entering markets in Pennsylvania, New Jersey, and Illinois following energy deregulation in those states. They were greenfields from a marketing perspective, since consumers had previously only been able to buy from their public utilities. They had not had any choice, and now, for the first time, they would.

There was a mad dash by many electric companies to enter these markets and get as many customers to sign up as quickly as possible. People were paying attention to the choices they had for the first time. They knew very little or nothing about any of the new companies offering to help them reduce their home electricity bills.

The company we worked with was not the largest player in the industry and did not have the biggest budget. They had to get creative in order to "punch above their weight" and make customers think they were large, trustworthy, and reliable.

The best way to gain a lot of awareness quickly is to understand the problems your customers are facing and speak to them. That year, gasoline prices were very high. It was putting pressure on household budgets and many were concerned about filling up their tanks and even taking road trips for summer vacations. The energy company we worked with was not in the gasoline business—they only did electricity. But they had a message about saving money that they wanted people to know.

They agreed to a campaign that helped people where they needed it most in order to create awareness for their brand. Their message was that they could help people save 10 percent on their home electricity bill compared to the public utility. The campaign was designed around the 10 percent message.

For a few hours in a very specific time period, the company offered to fill up people's gas tanks for just 10 cents a gallon. The event was promoted in advance using social media ads targeted to people in zip codes near the gas station. It was covered on the radio and in the news. While connected attention was not the goal, those who wanted to get the gasoline had to download a coupon in advance and use their e-mail address to do so. This gave the sales team some new contacts for follow-up after the event.

The day of the event, the local news came out and did stories about the promotion. The last time gas had been ten cents a gallon was decades earlier. They interviewed the company CEO. One news station even sent out a helicopter to show the line of cars waiting. Happy people shared photos and videos all over their social media channels, mentioning and tagging the company. The story got picked up by MSNBC.com and got the company national awareness. In one day, the company got 40 million new brand impressions, significantly more than any of the other competitors. They spent 6,000 dollars in gasoline to get it and a few hundred dollars in social media ads.

Not everyone was happy. Only 100 people could get the 10-cent gas and that meant many were not able to take advantage of the giveaway. There were some angry comments on Facebook. We were prepared for it and dealt with it by giving away some gift certificates for local businesses.

THE FIVE TYPES OF ATTENTION   9

There are always risks when it comes to increasing awareness exponentially. But if the company had not taken the risk, it would not have achieved the awareness it did and the market where the promotion was hosted would not have been the most successful new market launch in the company's history.

Connected Attention

Connected attention is an indication that an audience is interested in what you are saying or have to offer. They want to know more, though they are not ready for a conversation or a sales pitch. They are "just looking," to use a retail analogy. Connected attention is the secret to everything else you want to achieve with your marketing. It is the form of attention you can use to start supporting sales. If people want to connect with you, they will want to learn more. If you can give that information as they want it in a way that creates an emotional attachment to the company, the speed and efficiency from connected to converted can increase exponentially.

Getting connected attention usually requires an exchange of value. People want something they deem valuable in order to regularly give an organization their most valuable asset: their attention. For some brands, entertainment is enough. People follow them on Twitter because they are funny or witty. Sometimes deals get their connected attention. People know that every morning, there will be a new discounted or special item shared and the only way to know about it is to follow the company on Facebook. For some, news analysis is the reason to follow. People sign up to get an e-mail newsletter daily because there will be a collection of industry stories and an overview of what they mean. In the B2B world, access to insights or new ideas or to thought leadership will compel some people to download a white paper or an eBook in exchange for their contact information or some basic information about their role at their companies. At trade shows, people are often more than willing to leave their business cards in exchange for a stress ball shaped like a brain or, more recently, a small bottle of hand sanitizer.

The good news is that any form of marketing can be used to create connections. Advertising, PR, social media, e-mail marketing, event marketing, webinars, SEO, content marketing, you name it. The trick is to identify the perception of value each offers the audience with whom you want to connect.

The hospital and health care industry has become increasingly competitive in recent years. Hospitals need to make money, and the name of the game for most of them is loyalty. Since most patients do not pay for their own care—Medicare, Medicaid, or an insurance company does—they do not make decisions about care based on cost. Instead, they want to go somewhere they feel heard, cared for, and even loved.

A large hospital system came to us looking for connected attention. They had a huge population of patients and high levels of brand awareness; however, they interacted with most of their audiences once a year at most. They wanted to be the emotional choice every time a patient needed to find a new specialist, schedule a surgery, or have a baby. They wanted to be connected with people in all parts of their lives.

There were two primary tactics that worked for getting connected attention. The first was simple and easy to do. We created a weekly health and wellness related quiz on Facebook. Anyone who answered the quiz was eligible to win a gift basket of self-care products. The exchange of perceived value was simple. They had to give us their e-mail address in order to win the basket. The actual cost of the basket to the health care company was negligible. In many cases, the basket was full of samples they already had available for patients. In some cases, they added things that were relevant to an upcoming holiday like Christmas or Valentine's Day. The perceived value of the basket to patients, though, was high. They included all sorts of high-end products they could try for themselves—for free!

Similarly, the perceived value of giving their e-mail address to a hospital system they knew and trusted was low. Of course the patients would share it. In their minds, the hospital already had it (though not for marketing purposes), so they did not really think twice about sharing it again. For the hospital's marketing department, though, the value was incredibly high. They could not use patient e-mail addresses for marketing purposes unless they had consent to do so, and the sweepstakes gave them that.

Once they had the e-mail addresses, they could e-mail these people regularly, collect data, identify those most engaged, identify those not at all engaged, and improve their connected marketing efforts.

The added benefit of the campaign was that the hospital was actually educating the audience. They were also able to use social media advertising to target people who were not their patients but who lived in nearby areas. A little extra awareness never hurts.

The other way we formed connections with their patients was focused on leveraging the expertise of their doctors and making those doctors available online for free. We partnered with a local media company that provided journalists and hosts the opportunity to interview selected doctors via livestream. The hosts asked the doctors a number of precomposed questions about their practices, their innovations, and what they wanted patients to know. Patients could also submit questions in advance about conditions or concerns without including any identifying information. The hosts asked a few of the patients questions to make them feel heard and so people would log on to see the answers. People signed up to get a recording of the livestream—with their name and e-mail address—whether they asked a question or not. This was another way to connect with them. Finally, the recordings were edited and reused on the hospital's website and social media channels to generate even more awareness.

Many companies that are well-known in their industries lack connected attention. Everyone on the trade show floor knows them because they have been around forever as a major sponsor, but then a pandemic ends trade shows for a year. Or they have great foot traffic into their store for years and years. A flood happens and the store closes. Companies that have a strong social media presence with followers or a large e-mail list significantly mitigate these and other risks. They can turn to digital communications because they are able to do so. They have done the work: They have the marketing infrastructure they need to be dynamic and adjust to changes.

More importantly, companies that have connected attention are best positioned to get ongoing, repeatable, predictable engaged attention, which is invaluable.

Engaged Attention

If awareness is about creating an impression in the brain and connected attention is expressing openness to learn more, then it follows that engaged attention is all about starting a conversation. When people start to respond, it means that they have genuine interest in your brand or product and are getting ready to take actions that could grow your business.

One of our clients was an architecture firm celebrating its 50th anniversary. The company was well-known in its market and its industry. It built landmark buildings in New York City, Philadelphia, Atlantic City, and Washington, DC. Its work was respected for its design, its responsiveness to urban environments, and its ability to provide a return on investment for developers.

As architects, the talented people on the team were the most important factor for marketing the firm and selling to its clients. For that reason, we decided to make the 50th anniversary of the firm all about the future, not the past. Yes, there was a big party with clients, partners, centers of influence, and elected officials. But the main focus of the event was not a video or slideshow of biggest hits. It was the announcement of the first winner of the firm's student design competition.

Months prior to the event, we had understood that the firm needed fresh talent and wanted to be known for its support of emerging architects. We had also learned that architectural students needed paid internships in order to get licensed. The partners in the firm created a challenge. They chose a location for a potential building, put some constraints in place, and defined requirements for success. They set a deadline, and an internal team at the firm was chosen to judge the submissions. The prizes were set and for students, they were big: a paid summer internship and one thousand dollars went to the winner with smaller cash prizes for the second and third places.

While most students studying architecture east of the Mississippi knew the firm and some of its buildings, there were few connections and no engagement with this important audience. We crafted a promotional e-mail that we sent to heads of architecture departments and careers offices at selected universities. A social media advertising campaign was put into action solely targeted at current students studying architecture. A landing page was set up on Facebook to make it easy for students to submit their sketches in response to the challenge.

At the firm's 50th anniversary party, they introduced the future of urban architecture to their clients, partners, and friends. The first prize winner was offered an internship with the company, and when he graduated, he was given a full-time position. In a surprise move, the second-place student also received a paid internship and joined the firm for the summer. Both worked on signature projects for the company and became advocates for other students to join. Many promotional posts were created on social media about the winners, e-mails were sent to the firm's many different contact lists, and reporters even wrote stories about the winners.

The student design competition became an annual event. It changed over time from being an online event to an in-person one, and over the years interest grew both among the internal team at the firm and with students. Clients, partners, and centers of influence were excited to see the designs each year from talented new architects, and the firm benefited from all the engagement it received. It was possibly the best marketing campaign the company had ever done.

Engaged attention can come in many different forms and from many different audiences. The trick is to figure out what your business needs. For many businesses in the B2B industries, engagement is a measure of connection. Think back to the sales pretzel. Engaged audiences are the ones who have clicked on many e-mails, downloaded many white papers, signed up for many webinars, liked many LinkedIn posts, responded to surveys, or attended many events. They are people who stay connected over time and who have signaled more than once that they are open to conversations.

For business-to-consumer (B2C) customers, engagement shows up slightly differently. Often, it is in the form of someone asking a question online about a product, commenting on a social media post, clicking on an e-mail to visit a landing page, downloading a coupon, ordering a sample, or even putting something in a shopping cart. Of course, all these things are applicable to some B2B or nonprofit companies as well.

The hard truth about engaged attention is that companies in long sales cycles can spend years engaging with their customers before they ever move into the converted attention phase. For them, marketing is very different and it must be resourced differently. We will talk more about top-of-mind marketing in the audience section, but it must be the priority for companies where buying takes months or years. Top-of-mind marketing is a specific approach where the whole goal is to be there whenever someone is thinking about the products or the services you sell. Those who are steady win. Those who find many creative ways to talk about the same thing excel.

There are many other businesses—both B2B and B2C—for which targeted audiences are constantly sliding back and forth between engaged and converted attention. Someone buys something. That's great. But the future growth of the organization requires that they buy again and again and again. For certain marketing professionals, this is where the majority of their time and money should be spent: increasing the total lifetime value of a customer by achieving loyalty. Engagement is the only thing that matters in that situation.

We once hosted an event where one of the speakers was the CEO of a major convenience store chain. The company had high levels of awareness in most of its markets, it had a huge social media presence, lots of media coverage, and an enthusiastic employee base. He mentioned that the average customer visited his stores two and a half times per day. They stopped in the morning for coffee, grabbed sandwiches for lunch or dinner, and filled up their gas tanks. While he was pursuing new geographic markets, his priority was to increase that number and get more wallet share. That was the company's biggest growth potential, second to none. He just needed to keep their attention engaged.

Converted Attention

Giving Tuesday is the day every year that follows the biggest online shopping day of the year, Cyber Monday, which is only a few short days after Black Friday, a day best defined by people trampling each other to get a TV at a big-box store. A few years ago, some very smart nonprofit leaders decided to speak to the philanthropist in all of us and ask us to spend a little of our money helping others instead of buying yet another video game for our nephew who does not really like us anyway (that is not from personal experience!).

Recently, we were asked by a nonprofit organization that serves people experiencing homelessness to help them achieve their fundraising goal for *Giving Tuesday*. The first thing we realized was that it was the one day of the year when there would be the most competition from other nonprofits asking for money. Working with them, we extended the window of opportunity and began the campaign prior to Thanksgiving. The organization provided meals to many who would have otherwise gone hungry.

For weeks leading up to the holiday, we promoted a chance for people to sponsor a meal for another person. We pushed the effort through stories on social media and specific asks via e-mail. The local media covered the effort and let people know there was a small thing they could do to help others. Two days before Thanksgiving, the organization had achieved its fundraising goal.

A few days later was *Giving Tuesday*. We used some of the photos, videos, and stories from Thanksgiving to build on the momentum from that campaign. We also added in some new tactics, including a "never have I ever" prompt for interaction on Instagram. By the afternoon, the nonprofit had exceeded its fundraising goal for the day. Most of the donors donated for the first time. However, it was not the first time they had heard of the nonprofit. We had been working for more than six months to get awareness and connected attention before asking for donations.

There are very few situations where marketing can generate converted attention on its own. Online transactions are the most common way it can be done. In most cases, salespeople are involved in the process as well. That is not to say that marketing has no role.

Cass had the opportunity to sit on a panel at an event for inside salespeople. A large debate ensued about how to define a sales qualified lead as opposed to a marketing qualified lead. The truth of the matter is that it will change from company to company. The most important thing is that marketing and sales leaders within the company agree.

In cases where salespeople are responsible for converted attention, marketing must provide support. More specifically, they must help sales create a through-line from awareness to converted attention. Materials—including sales presentations, proposals, and case studies—must be provided to the sales team with messages and images that are consistent with a person's initial impression.

When an engaged prospect stalls in moving toward converted attention, marketing must also provide support to keep the communication moving. The PR team should provide recent news coverage of the company that can be sent to the prospect. The social media team should ensure that the prospect is getting paid ads on all social media channels. The e-mail marketing professionals should put the person on a segmented list of interested prospects to get messages about products, services, case studies, and events. We will talk more about this when we get to the chapter on surround sound, but getting converted attention is hard, and everyone must contribute.

Advocacy

Congratulations! Your targeted audience bought your service, accepted your job offer, donated to your annual fund, referred you a client, or bought your company. That is amazing! Now what?

Advocacy is the highest level of attention because it feeds all the other kinds. It is the kind of attention you get from people who are invested in your success and who redirect the attention that they are getting toward you.

There are two ways to generate advocacy: You can earn it or you can pay for it.

Influencer marketing has become all the rage in recent years. That is because some people have been able to get enough attention for themselves—mostly through social media—that brands are willing to pay to get some of it. For companies, this can be very effective. There are also some common pitfalls.

The best way to use paid influencers is to set a goal of getting awareness for your brand. That is achievable. The mistake many marketers make is thinking they can get influencers to sell their products. Just because lots of people love what an Instagram influencer wears or thinks a shirt is "fire" does not mean people will buy that shirt. However, you can certainly create an impression of your brand. You may even be able to cocreate content with an influencer that gets your brand in front of large audiences. If you run a contest or a giveaway with that person, you may even be able to collect some e-mail addresses and get connected attention. That is about the extent of what you can expect and it is important to plan your budget based on those realistic expectations.

That said, it is possible for you to find and get advocate attention from micro influencers. These are people who have small but very supportive and engaged followers. These people can convince others to support a cause, try a product, or eat at a restaurant. They will share information about your company for a free meal or an invitation to an exclusive event. For quite a few businesses and nonprofits, micro influencers are the best return on investment.

All influencers we have worked with agree on some common best practices:

- Trust that they know their audience better than you do and ask questions before sharing your plan.
- Do not dictate content; be open to their ideas and suggestions because they will likely come up with something better than your initial pitch.
- Support their efforts and cross-promote their content on your social media channels.
- Avoid the single post and try to create a plan with them that includes multiple posts, e-mail, landing pages, or other marketing materials.
- Give them something different or new. They are leaders and will not respond well to doing the same thing as everyone else online.

For many organizations, earned advocacy is the most important and effective way to get awareness, connections, engagement, and conversions.

Over the course of many years, we have asked business owners how they get new clients. Most of them say word of mouth. What does that really mean? It means that someone they know told someone else to consider doing business with the owner. Those middle people—those referral makers—have influence. People listen when they talk. They follow their advice. They do what they say. These referral makers are trusted. They are respected. And they are often overlooked.

If you rely on referrals, you have the attention of advocates. But we would bet that you have no plan to get more value out of those advocates or to create more of them. This is a mistake.

Most companies that rely on word-of-mouth referrals to grow their businesses invest the largest part of their marketing time and money into reaching customers. Why? We have no idea.

Getting and keeping referral sources engaged can be remarkably easy and rewarding, regardless of industry. They want to help you because they like you. They also want to be seen as smart, connected, and authoritative by people they know. Help them do both. Give them information, insights, early access to new products and services, samples they can try, the ability to partner with you on an event for your shared audiences, case studies of work you have done, or even a gift. A year-round plan to help these people help you may be the only kind of marketing you need to do if you do it well.

Generating advocacy from your actual clients and customers is the final way to get this type of attention. Testimonials, unboxing videos, and other forms of marketing content created by people who love you carry great weight with other customers. They have the added benefit of often being produced with great excitement and passion.

Generating customer content is harder and easier than it seems. For many organizations, customers are creating and posting content every day. Marketers are just not listening or looking for it.

Early in the 2020 COVID-19 pandemic, we hosted a webinar with leaders of arts organizations, including concert venues, theater production companies, and music producers. We were talking about engaging with their communities and their biggest fans without putting on live performances. Cass asked the attending organizations if they had collected Instagram photos and videos posted by others over the course of the previous year that they could use. Not one of them had done it. And yet when we looked at Instagram, there were dozens or hundreds or thousands of photos, depending on the size of the organization. It was so easy! They were all already out there on the Internet. They were not organized. They were not connected with an important message or call-to-action. They were not part of a marketing campaign. But they were there. More than they could ever possibly need were available. They just had to ask. And guess what? The people who posted them wanted to help. No one connected the dots that helping could be so easy. Permission was all that was needed.

Companies that try to get user-generated content without a plan, and often without an exchange of value, often fail. In the previous story, help-ing an organization you love is the value you receive. For influencers, they get the value of money or free stuff. But what about everyone else? Why would a regular person take a photo of our product in their home? Or a video for that matter? Before you create a user-generated content cam-paign to get advocacy, be sure to answer these questions. Very few people will do it out of the kindness of their hearts.

At the end of the day, successful businesses need all sorts of attention. But they do not need all the same types of attention at the same level at the same time. Focus on the types where you are lacking and you will find you get better results from the rest of your marketing efforts as well (see Exercise 1.1).

What Type of Attention Do You Need?
With 1 being the least, and 4 being the most...

How much awareness do you have?

| 1 | 2 | 3 | 4 |

How much connected attention do you have?

| 1 | 2 | 3 | 4 |

How much engaged attention do you have?

| 1 | 2 | 3 | 4 |

How much converted attention do you have?

| 1 | 2 | 3 | 4 |

How much advocacy are you getting?

| 1 | 2 | 3 | 4 |

In the next 12-18 months, what kind of attention will move the needle for your organization? (Pick One)

☐ Awareness   ☐ Converted Attention
☐ Connected Attention   ☐ Advocacy
☐ Engaged Attention

If you chose a type of attention further down the path, have you created enough awareness to support your priority type of attention?

┌─────────────────────────────────────┐
│   │
└─────────────────────────────────────┘

If no, how are you going to create the other types of attention to get the one you prioritized?

┌─────────────────────────────────────┐
│   │
└─────────────────────────────────────┘

Exercise 1.1 What type of attention do you need?

CHAPTER 2

The Six Audiences Who Matter

The People Whose Attention You Need

All marketing is about people. Actual human beings. They think, breath, eat, get stressed out, yell, laugh, and care about others. They have dreams. They want to succeed. They have fears. They want to avoid embarrassment. They are doing their best.

Too often, we think marketing is about creating exactly the right headline or image or webpage. We get so caught up in those things we forget about the people with whom we are trying to communicate. We forget that first and foremost, we need to get and keep their attention.

Attention for attention's sake is a farce. A company that provides financial consulting to businesses will not grow if it gets attention from gymnasts. Similarly, a company selling baseball bats will have no luck with soccer players.

Too often, we hear from business leaders who tell us that anyone can be their customer. While technically true for some, that approach to marketing is doomed to fail. Marketing to everyone means marketing to no one. There are very few situations in the history of humankind where a product or service can solve a problem every single human has. Of course, the COVID-19 pandemic in 2020 showed us one example, and companies who developed effective vaccines benefited. But for most of us not working to fight a highly contagious and deadly virus, we must focus our marketing efforts on the people most likely to want to hear what we have to say.

Before we dive into the six potential audiences your business may want to target, let us once again revisit what we know about humans. There are two ways to categorize them: demographics and psychographics.

Most marketing defines people by their demographics, which are characteristics often associated with objectively observable facts. Some examples of demographics include:

- Age
- Gender
- Race
- Income
- Education
- Location
- Religion
- Marital status
- Job title
- Number of children
- Pet ownership

These things can be helpful in determining what we know about the best audiences in order to easily locate others like them. However, defining people just based on their demographics misses their humanity. It also ignores the most powerful way we can connect with each other: through emotions.

Psychographics is the study of people based on their feelings, values, dreams, opinions, fears, beliefs, and attitudes. Understanding these helps us connect with our audiences much more fully. It significantly increases the speed with which we can get their attention because we can connect with something within them that is true and real. It helps us keep their attention because they feel heard, seen, and understood by communication that is meant for them and people who believe the same things they do. Examples of psychographics include:

- Values
- Fears
- Influences

- Concerns
- Dreams
- Information sources
- Brand loyalties
- Insecurities
- Stresses
- Joys

Quite often, we will find similarities in our best customers across all these different psychological characteristics. They value helping others or dream about owning their own businesses or struggle with addiction or really want the next promotion. Regardless of the audiences that are most important to growing your organization, it is critical that you know about their psychographics and demographics. Anything short of that will mean that your marketing strategy is largely uninformed, which will cause a real problem when it comes to developing messages and content.

But first, the audiences. Too often, marketing communications people are entirely focused on customers and clients. Those have historically been the most important audiences.

Later in the book, we share some thoughts on how to create alignment inside your business. The biggest challenge is pretty much always agreeing on the audience. Sharing all six options during those conversations will help identify underlying issues, concerns, and confusion. Choosing one and getting specific about those people will exponentially increase the effectiveness of your marketing.

There are three important caveats. First, marketing to one audience does not mean that you will offend another. You can choose messages, campaigns, and images that create an emotional connection with one group and barely register with another. That's okay. It's also okay if one group gives you a lot of engaged attention based on a campaign while you just get a little attention from another. That is the reality of making choices. And as the famous strategist Michael Porter says, "Strategy is about making choices along *many* dimensions, not just *one*. No single prescription about which choices to make is valid for every company in every industry" (Magretta 2011, 32). In other words, strategy is about trade-offs; it's about deliberately choosing to be different.

Another important caveat about prioritizing audiences is that it does not mean you have to be committed to that audience for the rest of history. No, the audience is going to change over time. Perhaps your company does not have the capacity to service all the demand in the market. It would make sense to change the focus from customers to potential employees for a time. The marketing plan might focus on promoting the best employees in order to get more of them. Would promoting your employees' stories and experiences offend your customers? Of course not! People love to work with companies that value their employees and showcase them.

The third important caveat when identifying and prioritizing audiences is focusing on those you want, not those you happen to have. We cannot express to you how many times we have been asked this question while helping companies define their targeted audiences. Some have a very hard time acknowledging that the people whose attention they have today are not the same people whose attention they are going to need to have in the future. It becomes easily apparent when they are defining the demographics and psychographics of an audience, and they start complaining. No one complains about their ideal audience. No one. If you find yourself or someone else talking this way, stop the conversation and refocus it on what you want. If the complaining continues, chances are that the person doing the complaining is not prepared to assist in the company's future growth.

Customers and Clients

Most marketing is focused on customers and clients. It pretty much always has been, and that makes sense because marketing mostly supports sales. Believe it or not, most marketers spend very little or no time talking with customers and clients.

We have never understood why customer service and marketing are separate functions within a business. The most important information marketers need to develop strategy include:

- What do customers care about?
- What problem are we solving for them?

- What do we do well?
- What do they wish we could do better?
- What do they say when they complain?
- What confuses them about what we do that we can make easier to understand?

All of this psychographic information is often held by customer service representatives or account managers. It is rarely shared with marketing, and when it is, it is usually in a very general report and only in companies large enough to have people dedicated to market research.

The good news is that social media has made it significantly easier for some marketers to understand customers because so many of them complain online. In fact, some large companies now have entire teams dedicated to customer service through Twitter. Those who work in those roles get first-hand experience with what works and what doesn't, what customers need and what they care about. The downside is that those jobs are often stressful and exhausting, particularly since people are willing to be angrier and more aggressive behind their computer screens. As a result, many people who work in those jobs burn out quickly.

Similarly, there are often big gaps between sales and marketing. Salespeople are notoriously bad at sharing information, leads, and success stories outside of "hitting their numbers." This does not need to be the case. We once knew of a marketing professional who made it her job to get to know a handful of the salespeople personally. She took them to lunch, hung out with them over coffee, and was even invited to listen in on their sales conversations with prospective customers. This made her the most informed person on her team, and she was able to develop some really innovative campaigns just by being the best listener. Likewise, we know of a business development person who realized the power of marketing to help him sell. He would send the marketing department doughnuts, comment on their LinkedIn posts for the company, and volunteer to help at trade shows. He had no trouble ensuring that he had marketing materials that spoke to his segment of the customer base.

Marketers and those responsible for marketing strategy aimed at customers really must focus on finding good stories from the best audiences.

These stories will help with all the types of attention necessary to move people from awareness to advocacy.

All marketing to clients and customers is about meeting them where they are. For a student loan company trying to get students to take or refinance loans, that was March Madness. For certain students at basketball-obsessed universities, most of which have large populations, there is nothing more exciting and no better time to express school pride. The company wanted to generate as much awareness as possible with the secondary goal of collecting e-mail addresses and getting connected attention.

In order to achieve the company's goals, our team knew we had to offer something with high perceived value. Utilizing the company's web-site, we created a landing page with an entry form where students submit-ted pictures of the "main street" on their college campus and their contact information in order to enter. The primary awareness drivers were social media ads and e-mail broadcasts done with a scholastic book publisher. Over the course of six rounds, different schools went head-to-head. People could vote once per day for the school of their choice in each matchup, and every time a school advanced, the cumulative prize increased. People whose photo won the most votes in the round advanced and received scholarships ranging from $100 to the grand prize of $2,150. The cham-pion was also able to donate $1,000 to the charity of their choice.

The campaign was incredibly successful. The day it launched, there were 28,000 visits to the website, the highest volume for a single day in the company's history. The website almost crashed. Overall, the campaign generated over 1,500 e-mail addresses of college students. The company also benefited from almost half a million brand impressions from college students and their social networks.

Employees

In recent conversations we have had with CEOs and leadership team members, their focus has shifted away from the customer audience being the priority. Many recognize that the growth they want to achieve is only possible if they have the right employees. A lack of employees is the single biggest thing holding them back. In many cases, they're turning away work from customers because they don't have the people they need to do it. This is particularly true in distribution, ecommerce, essential retail, technology, manufacturing, insurance, and professional services.

As a result, they are shifting their focus to employees. They must, for the first time in many cases, focus on getting attention for their company as an employer—not just as a product or service provider.

Creating an employer brand is not enough, though. You can absolutely be the employer of choice in your industry or geography, but if no one knows it, you will never achieve your goals.

Before you continue reading, know this: Building and promoting an external brand is not something that can be done alone. There may be some false starts and some barriers along the way. But there is a double benefit: People will want to work for you. And your customers will likely feel great about working with a company that cares about its people.

Traditionally, the human resources (HR) department is responsible for finding these new employees and helping them acclimate to the company. But there is a clear divide between HR and marketing, and that silo is what needs to be destroyed in order to recruit to fill the talent gap.

Before we go any further on the employee audience, we must share an important warning: successful employer branding requires that a strong, positive culture is already in place. If you are struggling with culture, please contact an HR consultant who specializes in that work. Marketing falsely to potential employees or creating a false perception of your workplace will backfire. Employees who take jobs will leave. Worse, they will let anyone who will listen know about their experience with your company.

Since most companies have never prioritized their employees as a marketing audience before, they need to understand their perceived company culture, where their strengths are, and what great stories they can tell. There are nine tools that can be used to determine how your employer brand is perceived:

- **Employee Survey**—We all know what this is. Make sure whatever you're using includes questions about how they describe the culture and whether they think it is an employer of choice. Also ask for specific examples of experiences they've had that demonstrate the culture. This will let you know if they are sharing genuine feedback, and these stories can become great content in the future.

- **Applicant Survey**—This is one of the most overlooked sources of information. People apply for jobs because they want to improve their current situation. Chances are, you already have a database of them with their e-mail addresses, the position(s) for which they applied, and their geography. Ask them a few questions either during the screening process or after about why they applied to work with you, what they think your culture is, and how they learned about the company. Sure, most of this will be complimentary since they want to work for you, but you will learn pretty quickly if there is a common perception that is not aligned with the image you want to convey.

- **Mission, Vision, and Values Worksheet**—This is not about whether your company has a written mission, vision, and values. You should already have those in place. Instead, you need to be clear about HOW you're delivering on those statements. What are the stories? How do you live these values? Who are the people who are the best examples of them? How well are your words becoming actions?

- **Online Reputation Audit**—Most people find open positions online. All people research companies online. So what does your online presence say about you as an employer? What copy, images, and videos are on your "About" and hiring website pages? What does your LinkedIn company page look like? What about the personal LinkedIn pages of your hiring and management team members? What about your other social channels? What about third-party websites? Have current or former employees written reviews on Glassdoor, Google, or Facebook that support or degrade your business? Has anyone else written about you as an employer? You need to know these answers to know how you are being perceived.

- **Awards and Recognition**—If you've won awards, what are they for and who gave them to you? More importantly, what other awards do you want to get in the future? Doing this work will help you realize how you want to be positioned in the market and who will give you credibility. Look at other companies who have received those awards to get some insight into who your competitors for talent are.

- **Champion Readiness Review**—Champions are your current employees who can become your ambassadors. We're going to talk about them more in the "Building the Team" section. But first things first: You need to identify them. Who are the people you want to showcase so you can attract more employees like them? Select a group of people diverse in age, background, and experience so that you can showcase the variety of people who will work well in your company. Also spend a little time thinking and talking about how ready this group of people is. Is there a person who is already a great writer? Already really good on video? Already a LinkedIn rock star? Already referring people to work at the company? These will be important factors as you think about training and deploying them to external audiences.

- **Diversity and Inclusion Commitment**—If you care about having a diverse workforce (however you define it), you need to carefully evaluate how effectively you are delivering on this promise. Do you have internal or external programs to attract and welcome employees who are different from your current staff? Are these programs well-resourced and effective? Or are they just lip service and everyone knows it? Where are the opportunities to improve?

- **Job Description Audit**—Most applicants will read a job description before applying. But most of them are bland and boring—sure, they may list the company values and some of the benefits, but they rarely communicate anything about the *feeling* of working there. Take a look at your job descriptions. What is the process by which they are written? What words are used effectively? What words and phrases are missing? If a potential employee only read this, what would that person feel about the company?

- **Content Review**—All companies today produce content. There are five types: written, visual, audio, video, and experiential. What does your content communicate? Is it aggressive? Generic? Warm? Exclusive? Technical? Does it help or hurt how you want to be perceived as an employer?

After you've done all this work, it's time to get the leadership, HR, and marketing teams together to review them. From there, there needs to be agreement on the types of employees you want to attract and how you're going to communicate externally to get their attention and leverage your company as the best place for them.

Deciding where to work is an emotional decision. According to hiring statistics provided by LinkedIn Talent Solutions (2015), the most important factors for accepting a new job are compensation (49 percent), professional development (33 percent), and work/life balance (29 percent). Each of these factors is emotional because each has a massive impact outside of the office. Compensation determines whether someone is able to send their child to college or go on vacation. Professional development determines how successful you can be and how far you can go in the company. Work/life balance is essential for mental health and burnout.

When getting attention for your brand as an employer, begin with the feelings you want your employees to have. Figure 2.1, adapted from

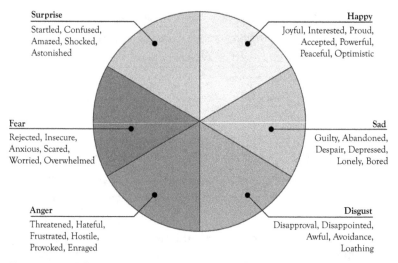

Figure 2.1 Wheel of emotions

Robert Plutchik's Emotion Wheel, (Hallett and Nguyen 2021) high-lights the most basic emotions, such as joy and anger, and then breaks them down further into more complex emotions. Debate the pros and cons of each one and how they fit into your business. At the end of the day, you should agree on three to five feelings you want to create. These become similar to values. The best companies will evaluate everything they do internally and externally based on whether they create these feelings. Every photo, every job description, and every social media post should help connect with potential employees emotionally. These become the "true north" for the employer brand and all attention will stem from them.

Centers of Influence

Earlier in the book, we shared some thoughts about advocacy as one of the types of attention you can earn. We mentioned that there can be great business impact from creating and executing marketing campaigns solely focused on referral sources. So how can companies attract awareness from centers of influence? The answer is top-of-mind marketing.

Think about the last time someone asked you for a referral. Perhaps they needed a new accountant or lawyer or massage therapist or land-scaper. What did you do? Chances are you thought of someone with whom you had a great experience or relationship. The experience could have been recent, or if it was truly spectacular, it could have been in the distant past. Most people suggest the one, two, or three companies that they think of first. Even if they had an amazing experience at a hotel on their honeymoon 20 years ago, they are more likely to recommend a hotel they stayed at more recently even if the stay was good, not great. That is because they have confidence it is still just as good as when they visited not long ago.

There are some basic principles for top-of-mind marketing that are required for it to be done well:

- **Simplicity**—If you are going to depend on someone else
  to get attention for your brand, it must be simple for them
  to explain what you do. Too often, companies try to

communicate all of their messages, as complicated and technical as they may be. While a customer might understand the nuanced difference between an electrical and self-actuated valve, the business coach carrying the message might not. Simple language, particularly when communicated in a single sentence, is critical for someone else to get attention on your behalf. Think about explaining your message to a fifth grader. Most newspapers are written at that reading level. That is because most adults can understand it even when the issue is complex or complicated. Some marketers argue that the integrity of the message can be sacrificed if simplicity is achieved. They may be right. But remember that awareness is not the only type of attention, and there will be opportunities to create engaged and converted attention once awareness exists.

- **Clarity**—In our example, the person asking for the referral is looking for the best options and turning to the trusted source because there is a perception that they know the best. The common next question is often about other providers. "Are they like [competitor A]?" "What makes them better than [competitor B]?" Your centers of influence need to be able to answer these questions in order to get you the attention you need. Creating a frequently asked questions e-mail that you send just to referrers every now and then can help with this, but so can conversations with your salespeople. Marketing can support sales here once again by using e-mail automation to set up regular networking calls and meetings with centers of influence. In those meetings, they provide a really clear and short document with just a few things they should know to make a great referral. They can also send those things as a follow-up e-mail so they are searchable and easy to forward to someone else.

- **Consistency**—Communication with referrers should not be limited to when there are gaps in the sales pipeline. There should be a plan in place to send them something new and different every few weeks. There should be intentional social media posts they can easily share. There should be events or webinars they can pass on to others. And there should be educational videos they can use to help others. All of these things arm people responsible for "word-of-mouth" with something more than some casual and unclear words.

- **Community**—The best way to get attention from someone else's network is to do something with them and form a shared community. Co-writing an eBook on shared areas of expertise, cohosting an event, having a referral partner on a podcast, or sharing a trade show space are all great ways to make it easy for others to promote you to their networks. Nothing says trust and credibility like partnering together to do something that helps you both.

In 2014, we began hosting Social Media Day in Philadelphia. It has become the largest event for digital marketing professionals in the area and has grown so much that it is now its own nonprofit organization. In the beginning, it benefited Slice Communications by helping us generate brand awareness for who we are and what we do. It also helped us get connected attention from people who signed up to learn more about it and of course, we generated quite a lot of engagement from people who attended. However, the biggest benefit we received is from our centers of influence. We have featured many of them as speakers, panelists, and moderators at the conference, which have given them reasons to promote us to their communities. Hopefully, we are also top-of-mind whenever someone asks them about a PR, social media, or e-mail marketing company. So far, the results prove that this works.

Investors and Donors

For some businesses, the most important audience is investors. These are the people who give you the capital you need in order to grow and thrive. Sometimes they are the people who buy your company. And sometimes they are the people who donate to your nonprofit. Of course, there are shareholders for publicly traded companies, but for the purposes of this book, we are going to focus on the first three mentioned since there are people much smarter about traditional investor relations.

Of course, you need to talk with your investors regularly. The best investors also become the biggest advocates. They benefit from you getting attention from other investors, customers, employees, and strategic partners. In all our years, we have never seen a marketer put together a plan focused just on investors. Some investors have marketers who develop plans to market companies, but not the other way around.

Many marketing plans aimed at investors can be similar to those designed for centers of influence. However, we recommend being more direct with investors. They can only win if they help you grow. We recommend developing a weekly communication to your investors with information about how investors can support you. For instance, let them know about an event you are hosting and ask them to invite people they know. Tell them about an employee that you want to hire, the qualities you are looking for in that person, and where you are looking for them. Share the job description of the posting that you are using to promote the job opening and ask them to put it on their social networks and e-mail newsletters. Figure out who your centers of influence are, whether the people who are referring business to you are attorneys, business coaches, marketing professionals, or consultants in other fields. Chances are your investors know some of them, so tell them that these centers of influence have been powerful forces for you growing your business and that you want to meet more people just like them. If there is one thing that we know about investors, it is that they are constantly surrounded by business consultants and people who provide professional services.

A long time ago, we worked with a health care client who was backed by venture capital investors; these investors also invested in other health care startups. Even though our client knew the industry, players, and many of the decision makers, they were still too hesitant to ask for the help they needed. They were too insecure to provide materials to the investors to help pass along information about who they were and how they could better serve patients. One day, they saw another company in the same investor's portfolio obtain a big media placement about a huge partnership with a hospital system. This made the client jealous, yet also caused them to decide to change their marketing plan to leverage the investor's clout. Things were never the same for that company as they realized that with the help and support of their biggest advocates, they could achieve their goals much more quickly and efficiently—all they had to do was ask. It also provided them—and us—with more deals and partnerships we could promote.

There comes a time in many business owners' lives when they decide that they want to sell their company. They have worked their whole life, invested blood, sweat, and tears into their business, and envisioned a future where they would be able to turn their investment in the business into cash to support their future retirement. However, selling a business is much harder than it seems. Marketing to potential acquisition investors— referring to those who have the cash to purchase a company and take on the future of that company—who have the skills and expertise to continue serving clients and the wherewithal to face the challenges that often come with acquisitions are the ones who are the hardest to find and most challenging to engage. Marketing a company for sale used to be the exclusive job of a business broker, but today acquirers find out about potential acquisition targets by reading the news, researching on LinkedIn, and signing up for newsletters to begin due diligence before they even inquire about the company. Even if a business broker is engaged, companies who are looking to acquire others will often check out the website, social media presence, other marketing materials, media coverage that has been generated, speaking opportunities that have been secured, and trade show presentations in which their potential acquisition targets are engaged. Business brokers value companies more aggressively when those companies have a large following, have an active segmented e-mail list, and have a highly engaged audience of influencers, referral partners, and customers. For all of these reasons, business owners who are close to exiting need to make marketing to investors their priority at least two years in advance of their intended exit.

Nonprofit donors and supporters are in a slightly different situation. First, it is important to realize that there are two different kinds of donors. There are large institutional and foundational supporters and smaller, individual supporters. The large institutional sponsors are always seeking good stories to share with their audiences as companies want to show that they are supporting their local communities and nonprofits. They need feel-good stories. They need amazing images. They need the opportunity to get in front of communities of people and showcase to them their corporate social responsibility plan. They also need opportunities to engage their employees to get them involved and provide volunteer events. Marketing to those groups means giving them all of the elements listed previously continually through the year. It also means documentation. It means calling them out on social media. It means getting them media placements for the work that they are doing in partnership with your nonprofit. These are all the things that they care about.

Foundations are a little different. Yes, they want great human-interest stories and to be able to showcase those things to their donors. In some cases, they like to put them out on their social channels. Still others, especially those that are family foundations, prefer to keep a lower profile. Marketing to them means one-to-one communication, such as individual e-mails and phone calls. It also means giving them full reports of how their money was spent. Those reports cannot just be program reports; they must be actual marketing materials. They need to make the case for not only why their money was well spent in the past, but why they need to continue investing in the future. These messages need to be reinforced through social channels so whenever they check them they see them. They also need to be reinforced on the website so when they show other people the website the messages are there. It is a slightly more nuanced marketing approach for this audience.

Keeping individual donors engaged and converted requires much more communication. First, they need to be well-recognized and personally thanked for their donations. You can often do that using e-mail marketing and e-mail automation techniques, but then, they need to have the opportunity to share information about you with others. Quite often, their motivation for donating is to feel good about themselves. Encourage them to follow you on Facebook or Instagram and ask them to leave comments. Let them know in advance about campaigns and fundraising efforts in which you are engaging. Make them feel part of the "In Crowd" by providing them with sneak peek and special event access. Send them e-mails every couple of weeks discussing the impact of their donation. Give them an opportunity to provide suggestions and make connections for you. Doing all of this will make them feel like part of the team. More importantly, it will create an emotional connection between them and the nonprofit organization, and there is nothing like an emotional connection to keep people converted.

Partners and Suppliers

Very few businesses these days go at it alone. Many have partners, suppliers, or they form joint ventures with others in order to market and sell their products most effectively. These three groups are incredibly important to the success of organizations, particularly in a market that is challenged by external and economic factors.

One brand that has generated significant awareness over the years is Intel. Intel has one of the most famous ingredient marketing campaigns of all time. They have worked with organizations like Dell, Hewlett Packard, and other computer manufacturers who invested heavily in marketing. Intel's approach was to support those marketing efforts and be included on television and in other advertisements. Intel knew that if they could associate themselves with these bigger consumer computer brands, they would be much more likely to create demand and awareness for their product and the value that it adds. However, they did very little marketing on their own outside of the computer industry. Today, many other companies model themselves after Intel's ingredient marketing campaign, and it works. Comarketing dollars, when spent well on a strategy that is aligned with an aware audience and with marketers who really have a focus on the impact they are generating, can provide significant returns. However, there has been a lot of competition for ingredient marketing because people know that it works efficiently.

So, how do you get a major brand who invests heavily in advertising to choose you for an ingredient brand for comarketing? It all begins with relationships. Relationships are not everything though, as you must also have a thoughtful, intentional, well-financed, and backed marketing plan to bring to these brands in order for them to choose you for an ingredient comarketing plan. This requires that you invest in your brand awareness so that major brands understand that you are not entirely dependent on theirs. You must be willing to push them to try new things and YOU must be willing to take the risks that they are taking. Finally, you must be willing to spend at least as much time cultivating those relationships as you are on the money for the ad spend.

Advertising is not the only place for comarketing today. Combined PR efforts where both brands together pitch a story to a reporter, promote new product development, and set a shared vision for the future are the ones that get the media coverage that makes a difference for both brands. There must also be crossover in terms of social media. That can be very complicated, particularly when there are other priorities for Facebook, Instagram, and Twitter pages. For that reason, social media is often the least effective comarketing platform. E-mail marketing cannot be over-looked when it comes to comarketing. Each brand should bring robust e-mail marketing lists that are highly segmented and targeted to the part-nership. Messages can go to both audiences and both lists and direct back to shared landing pages. The shared landing pages can have a contact form that leads to connected, engaged, and eventually, converted atten-tion. Doing that requires setting expectations around how these leads are managed, how they are reported, and how they are leveraged once a cus-tomer becomes converted.

One of the most important learnings of COVID-19 and the eco-nomic shutdowns that occurred as a result are the importance of commu-nication with suppliers. Many companies suffered because they were not able to obtain the supplies they needed to create their finished products. A great example is Pfizer, which had the ability to create a vaccine and produce it for millions of people in late 2020. However, they were not able to scale up their supply chain efficiently enough in order to meet the demand that existed for the vaccine. Many organizations struggle because they do not have connected and engaged attention from suppliers and potential suppliers.

As the leaders of a certified woman-owned business, we have had the opportunity to meet and speak with many people in Supplier Diversity and procurement at major companies over the years. One of their big struggles is finding enough small and small diverse businesses to supply their global operations. This is a two-way street, yet many small and small diverse businesses do not know how to market to large corporations. Cass has actually written an eBook entirely on that topic and all the digital dis-connect, which is available on Slice Communications' company website.

There is also a challenge for procurement professionals and supply chain professionals in terms of locating and identifying marketing to those who could supply them with the critical products and services that they need to make sure that their business continues to operate. They have had little to no marketing support. As a result, it is on their shoulders to research and find suppliers, but it does not need to be that way.

If instead they were to develop a marketing campaign that begins with generating attention and awareness from their potential suppliers, they would have the opportunity to build a robust database that is useful to them when it comes time to scale up quickly. They also need to communicate that their company prioritizes small and small diverse businesses. They need to communicate that to their primary suppliers so that those suppliers can go out and find second level suppliers that are small and small diverse. Many of these small businesses have products and services that could help these large corporations scale, but are not aware of their dedication to small businesses. They do not know the opportunity that exists and they certainly do not know how to stay connected and communicate with the suppliers when it comes time to try to source those goods or services. For some companies, this is the single most important aspect of being able to grow.

Competitors

Can competitors be a primary targeted audience? Of course they can, particularly in industries where innovation and user acquisition are the name of the game. In the private sector, think about startups that are entering a market dominated by large, multinational companies. We worked with one such company a few years ago. They had a really innovative product used for testing whether there was contamination in food products. Their intellectual property was well protected by patents. They had investors that were dedicated to their success as well as the support of the economic development and scientific communities in their area.

Consumer packaged goods companies, food manufacturers, wineries, and breweries all wanted the product because it was faster and cheaper than what the "big guys" could offer. Sure, our client wanted more customers, but sales was doing its job and the company was growing quickly.

What they really needed was attention from their competitors, because they knew that the competitors would be the most likely to buy the company for a higher price than a private equity group or some other acquirer.

For that reason, they focused on delivering their corporate message about their growth, their intellectual property, and their innovative discoveries through business media and speaking opportunities. They knew their competitors would be at all the same conferences they attended, so they needed a position of prominence to show they were to be respected. Getting coverage in major media, including *The New York Times*, demonstrated to their competitors and others in the industry that they had something truly differentiated to offer and that there was significant value in it.

At the end of the day, the company did sell to a competitor for a price that satisfied the founders, investors, and employees. They became a startup and venture capital success story in their area and their industry. They did this by prioritizing marketing communications focused on their competitors, which is not always the obvious choice.

When thinking about competitors, consider the five types:

- **Direct**—These are the companies that do basically the same thing you do for the same targeted audience. It can be very good to have direct competitors because they have proven a market and demonstrated a need for a product or service. Having a clear set of direct competitors can also make a marketing strategy easier to develop. It becomes easier to identify a customer audience when you know that those people are likely to be following or engaging with the competitor. It can be easier to develop a positioning strategy when it is clear which companies yours needs to position against. And in some cases, like the previous story indicates, it can be clear to everyone involved where there is an opportunity for acquisition. Of course, in some markets there are hundreds or even thousands of direct competitors, which can make positioning difficult. We recommend picking the three or four most prominent and focusing on them. Follow them on social media, sign up for their e-mail newsletters, put Google alerts on their company names and the names of their CEOs.

Doing all this will help inform your marketing strategy and ensure that it is adjusting to changes competitors and the market are experiencing.

- **Indirect**—There are companies out there that do something slightly different than what you do and are taking a share of the market from you. Our industry is a great example of that. We provide PR, social media, and e-mail marketing services. There are a lot of companies that provide website design, digital advertising, and search engine optimization. They do not do what we do exactly, but clients may decide to invest in a new website instead of spending money on social media this year. This is incredibly typical. It also makes marketing strategy a little more difficult because it requires education about what makes your products and services better than other, different products and services. There is an educational component that must be part of the plan when most of the competitors are indirect.

- **Perceived**—This is often the most overlooked type of competitor. These are companies that do not do what you do at all BUT customers and industry don't realize that. Imagine that you are in the compliance services business. No, most people don't know what that even means so don't overthink it. There is a perception that because compliance is a "legal thing," a law firm would be the best provider of these services. That is not the case at all. It is a different type of service that law firms don't do. In fact, they usually refer the business out to compliance service firms because they have no knowledge or capacity to handle the challenge of ensuring a financial services firm is compliant with regulations issued by the Securities and Exchange Commission. In complex and niche markets, perceived competitors are the most prominent and hardest to position against since there are extremely low levels of awareness and understanding.

- **Partner**—Partner competitors are the most common competitors for nonprofits. These are organizations that often work together to achieve a goal. Because they are achieving similar missions, there is competition for donors, both large and small. The same is true for organizations that depend on distribution partners or joint ventures. They work together sometimes, and they compete for clients, market share, and donations other times. This competitive landscape can be the toughest for a marketing strategy because it cannot put down the competitors, it cannot undercut pricing, and it cannot undermine the relationship. Instead, it must be thoughtful and supportive. Most often, we recommend a strong focus on creating engaged attention with audiences where partner competitors dominate the conversation.

- **Aspirational**—Many small and emerging companies are not even considered to be on the same level as their competitors, but they want to be. Identifying a clear set of organizations that you want to compete with can give the marketing team a very clear direction and make decisions about the marketing strategy easier. Often, the focus of this strategy is all about awareness from the aspirational competitors' audiences. The good news is that "punching above your weight" is very doable from a digital perspective where the playing field tends to be more level and a company can make steady progress running toward the end zone.

Over the years, we have worked with more than one CEO who has told us that their company is so innovative and different that they do not have competitors. They are lying to themselves and others. There is no such thing as an organization that does not have competitors. If you are having a hard time figuring out who your competitors are, ask these questions:

- Who is getting the attention I want to get?
- Who is getting the money I want to get?
- Who is getting the credibility I want to get?
- Who is getting the thought leadership recognition I want to get?
- Who is getting the speaking opportunities I want to get?
- Who is getting the referrals I want to get?

If nothing else, you have competition for attention. Once you understand this, developing a plan that gets that attention will be much easier (see Exercise 2.1).

Which Audience Is Your Focus?

Which audience is the most important to your business in the next 12-18 months?

☐ Customers/Clients   ☐ Partners/Suppliers
☐ Employees   ☐ Investors / Donors
☐ Centers of Influencer   ☐ Competitors

What do you know about their demographics?

Job Title: _____

Company: _____

Age: _____

Family Situation: _____

Geography: _____

Educational Background: _____

What do you know about their psychographics?

Fears/Concerns: _____

Aspirations: _____

Pressures: _____

Where they get news and information: _____

How they make decisions: _____

Who influences their decisions: _____

What type of attention do you need from this audience?

☐ Awareness   ☐ Converted Attention
☐ Connected Attention   ☐ Advocacy
☐ Engaged Attention

What do you need to learn about your audience to more effectively get their attention?

_____

Exercise 2.1 Which audience is your focus?

CHAPTER 3

Messaging at the Core

Centering on What People Need to Know

The biggest mistake we have seen companies make over and over again when it comes to messaging is that they make their messages all about them. This is wrong. Messaging should always be focused on the highest priority audience. Effective messaging is not about what you want to say; it is about what the audience wants to hear.

At our agency, we work with every single client at the beginning of every engagement on their messaging. What they say often determines whether they get the type of attention they need to grow. However, very few of the companies we work with have thoughtful, intentional messaging in place. Instead, they just have the bullet points the sales team uses or the headlines from the website. Often, these have either been done in a complete silo, as is the case with the sales presentation bullets, or they have been done by committees in the case of the website headlines. Either way, they are developed by people who are not marketing professionals, who have not put the audience at the center, who have not considered the competitors, or who have not tested the messaging. Let us review each of these common messaging mistakes and how to overcome them.

The biggest push-back we often receive from clients when we begin audience-centered messaging is that everyone is their audience. This approach will sink a marketing strategy before it even takes shape. That is because when you try to talk with everyone, you end up saying nothing to no one. Of course, there are brands like Coca-Cola that try to speak to every person on the globe. They also spend $4 billion annually on advertising. If you don't have $4 billion to spend on marketing, you should not follow their strategy.

Most organizations do not have unlimited time and money to spend on marketing. That is why we need to make choices and focus.

When you begin to engage in audience-centered messaging, you should find that it is easier than you thought because it requires you to communicate a few things, not everything. Of course, there are always those people who want to communicate everything all the time and are not satisfied with a marketing plan unless it includes every single feature and benefit. The problem with those people—and we can confess to having those tendencies—is that they overwhelm their marketing teams and the audiences that are most likely to contribute to their growth. They also do not get the results they want because they have muddied or confused their messaging. There is just too much communicated, and as a result, nothing has stuck with the audience.

We have also repeatedly heard the objection that if messages are designed for one audience, other audiences will be alienated. That is rarely true. We have never worked with a company that developed messages for customers that offended investors. Nor have we worked with an organization that had messages for donors that upset vendors. It just does not happen.

There is one important caveat. On more than one occasion, we have worked with a company that put messages into marketing aimed at customers or investors that the employees did not believe. In some cases, they were overreaching. In others, they were promising a product or service that was not ready and that the employees did not believe could be ready on time or within the budget. Most companies are not led by people willing to so grossly misrepresent their capabilities. However, overpromising or being hyperbolic in your messaging can hurt the company and undermine trust from employees.

All of this said, do not let fear of offending one audience get in the way of developing and delivering messages aimed at the people most likely to help you grow. The best examples of this are companies who deliver messages about how they help their audiences. Sometimes that means solving the problem of lost inventory or crow's feet lines around the eyes or making a low-risk investment or providing additional services through a partnership. Sometimes it means helping them achieve their goal of having a dream wedding or getting promoted or helping to feed hungry people or jointly developing a new cancer treatment.

Chances are that when you read that last paragraph about solving problems or achieving goals, you felt something. And it is even more likely that you had more positive feelings about the achieving goals examples.

The most effective audience-based messaging is either visual or visceral. It either helps them see something or feel something. According to *Encyclopedia of Distances*, by Michel Deza and Elena Deza (2009, 155), "Visual thinking, also called visual/spatial learning or picture thinking is the phenomenon of thinking through visual processing. Visual thinking has been described as seeing words as a series of pictures. It is common in approximately 60–65% of the general population."

Most people turn words into pictures. It is how they understand concepts, opportunities, and of course, messages. However, most messages do not make this easy. They are too complex and too filled with jargon for a person to be able to understand them in a series of pictures. The best messages make it easy. They create similarities to what people already know and can already see. Once a visual thinker can see the benefit the company provides in their mind's eye, they are much more likely to remember it and envision themselves receiving the solution or accomplishing the goal.

The other way to make a message memorable is to create a feeling. A quote attributed to Maya Angelou, though there is debate about this, reads, "I've learned that people will forget what you said, people will forget what you did, but people will never forget how you made them feel" (quoted in Deutsch 2014). Regardless of the origin of the quote, the sentiment is right. Feelings stick with human beings. Decision makers, even in the most technical, the most mechanical, the most bureaucratic positions, are human beings. They feel. Messages that give them a feeling will be ones that they remember.

We have a saying at our company: Different is better than better. The second messaging mistake that companies often make is saying the same thing as their competitors. Often, this is caused by a lack of knowledge about what is being said outside of the company's walls or in the marketing.

When Cass was growing up, she spent a lot of time with her grandmother, known to most as "Grammy." Grammy was a remarkable woman who survived the Great Depression, World War II, boarding school with Catholic nuns, the 1960s, domestic violence, and six children. She had a high school education, ran purchasing at General Electric's West Philadelphia plant during the war, drove a school bus for differently-abled children for more than 20 years, and read multiple newspapers every day.

Grammy was an adventurous woman. She would pile Cass' brothers, some of her cousins, and Cass herself in her very small car and start driving. The children were fortunate to attend performances by the Philadelphia Orchestra, visit Native American reservations, tour the local TV station, and do all sorts of other things that are not typical for children in the New Jersey suburbs. Sometimes these adventures were amazing, opening their minds to new possibilities and opportunities. Sometimes they were duds or even disasters. In those cases, Grammy would always end the day with one of her classic sayings: "At least it was different."

Cass learned the inherent value of "different" from her grandmother at an early age, and it is one of the many lessons she applies to running Slice Communications. It is also a fundamental way she approaches messaging.

The first key to differentiating is understanding context. Just saying something different than what your previous messaging had been will not work. Instead, you need to understand the external. What is the status quo? What are other companies saying? What is everyone that matters thinking or talking about? These questions must be answered before differentiation can be established. Research must be done, analysis should be conducted, examples must be shared. This can be a lot of work, depending on the size of the landscape. But it must be done every year or more often if there are a lot of changes, new players, mergers, or acquisitions. Without it, you cannot know if what you are saying is truly different.

The second key to differentiating is identifying provable facts. Many companies say that "it's our people," that makes them different. Did you notice the first word there? Many. Many, many, many companies say that. Is that different? No! Is it provable? No! Whatever it is that you are saying makes you different must be objective and independently observable. Otherwise, it will not ring true.

One of the big challenges many small businesses have is that they do not have a clearly differentiated product or service. They can unclog a drain or sell a pair of shoes or make a sandwich or print a brochure or do a tax return. In these cases, there may be a provable difference if you look hard enough. They may guarantee the drain remains unclogged for a year. They may offer sizes of shoes no one else does. They may make the sandwich with ingredients from farms within 10 miles. They may print within two hours of the order. They may do very complex tax returns that others cannot. All of these are provable differences that exist.

Sometimes, the provable differentiators do not yet exist, but they could. This is where marketing can and should influence the business. Imagine there is a dry cleaner. They do the same thing as every other dry cleaner. They are open the same hours, have the same turn-around time, have roughly the same pricing, and so on. There is nothing different about the way it operates, and so marketing is going to be very difficult. There are a few approaches this company can take. One idea is to change its chemicals and processes so that it is environmentally-friendly. That may really resonate in some geographic areas or with certain audiences. Another idea is to add shoe shining to the services so that customers can make sure their clothes and shoes are clean and look great without an additional stop. Another idea is to add curbside delivery so the customers do not have to look for parking or get out of the car. Another idea is to be open on Sundays when no one else is. Or to offer laptop cleaning services in addition to dry cleaning. Or to provide at-home stain treating samples for every new customer. The list can go on and on. Yes, some of these ideas cost money. Some of them can make money. The bottom line is this: If you do not have a differentiator, but you still want to get a lot of attention, you need to create one.

Unlike the aforementioned example, there are times when a company's offering is so new and so different, people have a hard time contextualizing it at all. A marketing trick we employ in these cases is to create a new category. We worked with a really cool startup that had software and robots that would roam a grocery store and let the workers in the store know when products needed to be restocked. The problem was simple: Grocery store managers were inefficient in allocating their teams to restock, leaving some product areas completely empty. This reduced revenue because items that could have been sold were sitting in the storage area. There was also a really clear fear: That robots would take the jobs of the grocery store workers. Because this was a totally new and somewhat scary product, we decided it would be best to create and name the category. That way, we could communicate the context and then position the company inside of it.

"AI" is often understood as "artificial intelligence." In most business settings, it is considered transformative, efficient, and advanced. It is associated with cost savings, better insights, and real-time decision making. With this in mind, we created a category we called "aisle intelligence." It provided all the benefits of AI in the retail aisles. The term had never been used before, and yet it was memorable, communicative, and differentiated. It gave visual thinkers a picture to consider because they likely already had a picture of AI in their minds. Because it was new, we were able to purchase a domain name associated with aisle intelligence for our client. As a result, the company was able to more clearly communicate what it did to customers, investors, centers of influence, partners, and employees. All of this power came from naming a new category that in and of itself was different.

The last messaging mistake people make over and over again is not testing the message externally. It does not matter that everyone at your company can repeat the messaging verbatim in their sleep if they do not work for others. We are big proponents of market research, but a full research program with focus groups, surveys, and qualitative testing is not always necessary. If the primary audience is customers, have your sales team create a new slide in their deck or a new sentence in their proposal where they try the new message for about a month. Every time they give that presentation or review a proposal, ask them to fill out a quick form with feedback. You can do the same thing with investor presentations if you are raising money. Make it easy and make it consistent, and you will get a lot of what you need to know without a big investment. This methodology will also help you combat a message you know is wrong or a person whose opinion of the new message is misguided (see Exercise 3.1).

See, it can be pretty quick and easy. Just do not ask too many questions or you will lose the cooperation and involvement of the sales team. They have quotas to achieve and numbers to hit, and they cannot spend too much time responding to marketing's requests. If you make it easy and are clear that better messaging will lead to more attention, which will lead to more opportunities for them, you are likely to get just what you need for informed and targeted messages.

Sales Team Messaging Survey

Use this survey to leverage your sales team in message development. To best use it, give a copy of this survey to your team for any prospect or client calls, and ask them to complete it as soon as possible after the call.

Did the client or prospect understand the message?
☐ Yes, they seemed to grasp   ☐ No, they asked lots of
   it quickly   questions or needed me
                                               to repeat it

Was the client or prospect able to repeat the message back to you?
☐ Yes   ☐ No   ☐ Not sure or didn't
                                                             ask

Did the client / prospect understand how we're different?
☐ Yes, they mentioned   ☐ No, they asked   ☐ Not sure or didn't
   one or more of our   lots of questions   ask
   differentiators back   or needed me to
   to me   repeat it

Did the client / prospect use any words or phrases about what they need / desire that could inform our messages? If yes, please include them.

```
┌────────────────────────────────────────────────┐
│                                                  │
│                                                  │
│                                                  │
└────────────────────────────────────────────────┘
```

If this was a sales presentation, did they want to know more?
☐ Yes, they asked follow up   ☐ No, they asked lots of
   questions and wanted   questions or needed me to
   additional information   repeat it
   it quickly

Any other thoughts or notes from the call?

```
┌────────────────────────────────────────────────┐
│                                                  │
│                                                  │
│                                                  │
│                                                  │
└────────────────────────────────────────────────┘
```

Exercise 3.1 Leverage sales team in message development

Another simple way to test messaging is to either use social media or e-mail marketing. Let's start with social media. Create some graphics or some posts with the new messages. Use a few dollars on Facebook or LinkedIn to put that message in front of people likely to be your targeted audience. See how many people click it, leave a comment, like it, or have some other interaction with it. Try a few different images, a few different words or phrases, or slightly different targeting. Even this simple and inexpensive exercise will give you more information than you have now.

Similarly, e-mail marketing can give you insights into which message-containing subject lines get people's attention, which messages make them click, and whether there are other interactions based on particular phrasing or images. Be very careful, though. In order for this to give you valuable data, you must send the message-testing e-mails to the right people that represent your highest priority target audience. If your e-mail list is a mish-mosh of lots of different contacts collected over years without any curation, you are likely to get bad data. If you have a segmented list of people who have applied for jobs and your target for messaging is potential employees, you are on the right track. Remember that your e-mail marketing is only as good as your e-mail list.

When evaluating a message, the question is not whether or not someone likes it. That does not matter at all. Instead, messaging has a job to do. Here are the requirements of an effective message:

- **Communicative**—When you share the message with someone outside your organization, do they understand it? Does it communicate what you want it to? What do they think it means? Is it clear how you can help them and benefit their lives or workplaces? If a message does not clearly communicate a concept, visualization, or feeling, it is not a good message.
- **Memorable**—We explored earlier two different ways to ensure that a message is memorable: It should be visual or visceral. However, no matter how visual or visceral you think it is, it may not be that way for others. The trick is to make it simple enough that they can share it with others accurately without interference from you. Think about a marketing mes-

sage you have experienced lately that was memorable. What about it made you remember it all these hours, days, weeks, months, or years later? Apply that experience to the messages you develop.

- **Differentiated**—We have spent a good bit of this chapter already talking about differentiation, so we will not go too much further into detail. When evaluating a message for differentiation, the most important thing is to be honest with yourself and others on the team. Do not make the mistake of fooling yourselves into believing that you are communicating something different when you know deep down, you are not. Challenge yourself and others. If the message is not different, add something to the company that is, or create a new category.

- **Intriguing**—Effective messaging gives people just enough information to make them want more. They request it because what they have heard, seen, or experienced something that has intrigued them. That is ultimately the job of great marketing messaging. It makes people start to sell themselves.

If your new messages check all four of these boxes, you are well on your way to getting the types of attention you want and need from your targeted audiences. If not, keep working or get some outside help for a fresh perspective.

Before we go on, a word about wordsmithing. Message development is not about a quest for the perfect words. It is about concepts. We once worked with a CEO who spent weeks upon weeks going through dictionaries and thesauruses looking for the exact perfect words that communicated everything he wanted to communicate. He never found them because they did not exist. They rarely do. All he did was delay the marketing communications strategy by six months. He refused to put anything out into the market until it was perfect. It never was perfect. That is the frustrating part about communicating. It is rarely perfect. Can you think about a time when you perfectly communicated exactly what you wanted to say without any uncertainty or rephrasing or paraphrasing or pauses? Neither can we. But we certainly have had times that we communicated effectively with words, body language, images, and stories. We are sure you have too.

Now that we have explored messaging mistakes and requirements, let's dive into the three types of messages every organization needs. Together, these form the three legs of a marketing communications strategy. Everything else is built on them. They form the basis of all content, all PR, all social media, all e-mail marketing, all advertising, your website, your billboards, your brochures, your sales presentations, and the list goes on.

Positioning Statement

What is your position in the market? Well, it depends—and it will and should change to meet the market.

We start at the beginning with the type of attention you want to get. If your goal is awareness, you will likely want to have a broad positioning statement that attracts the attention of a lot of people in your target market. If you are focused on getting converted attention from lots of people who already know you, are connected with you, and are engaged with you, it may be different. That is because there is already so much they know, as opposed to audiences that have no awareness or know very little.

The second question to ask is who is the audience for whom you are developing a positioning statement? Investors? Employees? Existing customers who have not bought anything in a while? Referral sources who need to advocate to their contacts for you? Your positioning statement should be a single sentence that clearly and memorably communicates what makes you different. It is really hard for most organizations to do this work. A linguistic tool we often use is the "first or only" statement. Consider this: _____ (your company name) is the first/only _____ (noun).

If you can simply and easily fill in those blanks without any other thought or work, congratulations! You can move into the next phase of messaging. Unfortunately, most organizations do not fit into the category of truly "first" or truly "only." Instead, they need modifications, additional information, or clarification.

Here are some other exercises you can explore with your teams to identify the foundation of your positioning statement:

- The one thing about us that will get the most attention from the right people is: _____.
- Unlike _____ (primary competitor), we deliver _____ (benefit) to _____ (target audience).
- If our competitor were to buy us tomorrow, they would get these things they do not currently have (provable facts): _____.
- In the future, we will meet _____ (targeted audience's) needs in this new and different way _____.
- _____ (target audience) cannot live without us because we are the only ones who can _____ (provable fact).
- If I were to wave a magic wand, we would be different in this way: _____.

All of these different exercises will give you bits and pieces of information you can use to craft a positioning statement. Now, of course, comes the hard part. In 1750, the great Philadelphian Benjamin Franklin wrote to the Royal Society in London, "I have already made this paper too long, for which I must crave pardon, not having now time to make it shorter" (Revolutionary War and Beyond n.d.). Making the statement as short as possible without losing the meaning requires the skill of a marketing person or team. It is their job to take all the possible ways a company takes a different approach and simplifies it into something that can be easily communicated by all.

That may seem like a lot of pressure on one sentence, but keep in mind that a positioning statement is just one leg of the stool. It almost always works in conjunction with a point of view and supporting messages. They complement each other by building on each other. So do all the work you need to do to ensure that the positioning statement is as good as it can be. Then take a step back and evaluate it in conjunction with the rest of the messaging trifecta.

Before we go on, a word about adjectives. You will notice that in all these exercises, we focus on nouns and facts. That is because adjectives are nothing more than crutches holding up messages that are not truly differentiated. They are cheater words that every human over the age of seven can easily identify as marketing fluff. The more you can stay away from the "sizzle" and deliver on the "steak," the better off your company will be.

Point of View

Many people today work with organizations who believe the same things they do. However, most companies never take the time to articulate their beliefs. This is a lost opportunity to connect with a targeted audience on an emotional, human level.

A point of view is different from a mission statement or corporate values. This is about the organization's world view, how things should work, how business should be done, how life should be lived, how experiences should be experienced. What does your company believe?

For some, the point of view is at the heart of why they exist. They can easily fill in this blank: We believe that _____.

For many others, it is much harder. In particular, companies that are in commodity industries often were not founded to, or aimed at, making the world a certain way. They exist to sell stuff. However, a point of view can be the primary differentiator in industries with little or no differentiation. Would you rather buy widgets from a company that exists to sell widgets or from a company that exists to make the world's most sustainable widgets? Would you rather buy gadgets from a company that manufactures the most gadgets or from a company that uses gadget-making as a way to employ people in impoverished communities?

Take the example of Toms. Cass does not particularly like their shoes. She finds them uncomfortable. But she has a pair. So does her daughter. So does pretty much every woman she knows in her age group. Why? They are not cute, though the new line of boots caught Cass' eye recently. She has them because she knows that for every pair she buys, one is donated to someone who needs shoes. They believe that every person should have shoes on their feet. We both believe that too.

Toms calls themselves "the original One for One® company." They created the category and as you can see, registered a trademark for the category. Do you know how many other shoe manufacturers there are in the world? Neither do we. But we bet if you asked most people under a certain age, they would know Toms and what they believe. They would know that the company stands for everyone having shoes.

So what is it that your company believes? Here are some sample statements you can use to uncover the point of view:

- At the end of the day, the world is a better place because our company: _____.
- If there is one thing I want everyone to know about why _____ (company name) exists, it is: _____.
- Our customers keep working with us because they also believe: _____.
- When I die, I want to be remembered as the business leader who made our industry better by: _____.
- At the end of the year, we need to have done this one thing to improve our entire market: _____.

Once again, the marketing professionals need to collect all this information and turn it into something that is communicative, memorable, differentiated, and intriguing. It should be one simple sentence with the fewest words possible.

Supporting Messages

Supporting messages are the last leg of the stool. They are the three to five most important things an audience needs to know in order to do business with you. Once again, they should be fact-based, not full of flowery language that means nothing.

Put yourself in the mindset of your most important target audience. What are the things they absolutely need to know about you in order to ask for more information? Here are some supporting messages that are often wastes of communication:

- How long your company has been around/when it was founded.
- Your company's founding story.
- How many years of experience your employees have.
- How many awards you have received.
- How many customers your company has.
- Product features.

Most of these are what we call "vanity messages" because someone in the organization thinks they are important, but the targeted audience could not care less. Instead, focus on the three things that really matter to them and make those statements as simple and clear as possible. If you can, make them visual or visceral.

McKinsey has a concept called MECE, which "is essentially a thought-process that keeps ideas from getting muddled up" (Gaurav 2016). It stands for Mutually Exclusive, Collectively Exhaustive. We have found this principle very helpful for evaluating the messaging trifecta once a draft has been created. Do the positioning statement, point of view, and supporting messages work together without overlapping? If there is overlap, where and how can it be edited out? Each piece has its job, so there should be no part of the messaging doing the job of another part. Second, if you effectively communicate all the parts of the messaging, is it enough to get the attention you need? If not, what is missing? Where can it be worked into the trifecta? Once you and your team are satisfied that your messaging is MECE, it is time to start articulating it through content.

CHAPTER 4

The Five Types of Compelling Content

How to Change Your Ideas Into Content

Storytelling is one of the most powerful ways we communicate with one another. Everything we do is based on stories we tell—both to others and ourselves. In recent years, there have been books, speeches, and full-blown marketing courses that claim that content is king. What this really means is that storytelling is king. Because when created and disseminated strategically, content can effectively transport an audience through a full range of emotion and understanding—including moving them through the different types of attention. Content brings your story to life. And while we'll cover all of the content tools at your disposal in this chapter, written content tends to be particularly adept at accomplishing the art of storytelling.

Written Content

When most people talk about content, they are referencing books, blog posts, white papers, e-mail copy, social posts, press releases, and so on. This book is a form of content because it has ideas in it that we are sharing with you. People receive information efficiently through reading, and many enjoy doing it because it's a very self-directed process that enables people to get as much (or as little) as they want out of the material. It is also a very transferable form of information gathering, with one click of the "share" button on LinkedIn, and it's easy to reference written work when speaking with someone. Not to mention, search engines love written, keyword-rich content.

There are downsides, however. Most people find it very hard to write consistently, if at all. It can be overwhelming to stare at a blank screen and decide where to begin. It's intimidating to conceptualize topics and then fulfill them in a way that is interesting all the way to the last words. There is a real fear of writing that exists in many people.

The good news is that there are many new approaches to writing that can make it easier. Part of this book was written using Google's talk-to-text function. For Cass, when her shoulders got tight and fingers sore after hours of writing, she turned to voice typing in Google Docs. Of course, she had to go back and edit the text, but the talk-to-text function gave her a way to get her thoughts on paper and move the narrative forward through writer's block. Sometimes it's just easier to talk than to write.

In 2020, we also began a process whereby we would film quick videos on a topic that were then used as the basis for ghostwriters to draft blog posts under Cass' name. Many other CEOs have started adopting this approach. It has the twofold benefit of resulting in both written and video content with very little additional work on the part of the content originator. Still, if you are struggling to find the words, remind yourself to frame it like a story. Who are you telling this story to, and why?

One of our nonprofit clients tasked us with creating a fundraising campaign around the holidays—the very same organization that utilized our "never have I ever" campaign from Chapter 1. As anyone with an e-mail address can attest to, it's hard to break through the noise of "asks" during the end-of-year giving season. Again, this particular nonprofit serves people who are experiencing homelessness, so rather than write a series of posts asking for funding to support their great work, we took a step back. Who were we speaking to and why? We were directing these social posts and e-mails to a community who has already engaged in some way, whether they have volunteered in the past or just signed up to receive e-mails. They know in theory about the good work that's being done. We needed to communicate the real value they, as donors, can provide, and showcase the real-life impact. So we created written spotlights of guests who used and appreciated the organization's services and we helped tell their stories. How had this organization changed their lives and helped them when they needed it most? These moving stories addressed the "why" of it all, and without capturing these words in writing, the real message may have been lost.

The same written storytelling approach can and should be applied to B2B industries as well. Think about the clients you've helped, the problems you've solved, the growth you've enabled—and tell those stories in case studies. Written content can be so relatable, we just need to give it the time and space to resonate with our key audiences.

If you still find yourself strapped for time, there are a number of content creation professionals who can be employed either as full-time, in-house team members or as agency partners. They write for a living and know lots of tricks to make it as easy on the idea-creator as possible. If you provide direction, they can put pen to paper on your behalf.

Written content, however, is only one aspect of a content marketing strategy. The other four formats that should be considered are visual, video, audio, and experiential (see Figure 4.1).

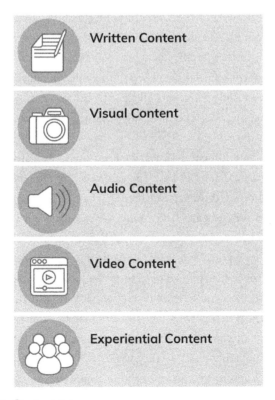

Figure 4.1 Content types

Visual Content

A picture is worth a thousand words, right? Think about the power of creating meaningful content that is communicated through still images. As mentioned previously, 60 to 65 percent of people are visual thinkers. They like to see pictures that they can relate to and remember, from the artfully composed work of a photojournalist in the field to a pie chart that translates complicated data into something more accessible. Both of these examples tell stories and can elicit emotion, just like writing. A behind-the-scenes photo from your company's fundraiser, a well-designed logo for your newest initiative, an infographic demonstrating your company's growth: All of these are visual content, and all companies can produce them.

Be warned, however: Running with the first search result from a stock photo website may check the box for visual content, but it may not add value. Ask yourself again what you're really trying to communicate and what you need this visual to accomplish. When working with a global manufacturer, we were tasked with promoting their sustainability report. The results were objectively impressive, with the company having made massive year-over-year improvements in reduction of emissions. The first choice in visual content was a simple pair of hands holding a green leaf: a symbol of nature and environmentalism. The call to action was to download the full report. Was it aesthetically pleasing? Sure. But it didn't convey the significance of this milestone. Instead, we opted to create a series of simple but bold infographics that each featured one statistic from the report in an easily digestible way. The call to action remained the same, but the visual directed the tone of the report and demanded a bit more attention from the audience. The result? The company saw an impressive increase in year-over-year engagements with their sustainability content.

Similarly, we worked with a recruiting firm in the past whose real differentiator in the industry was their employees. Time and time again, their clients came back because of the customer service and expertise offered by the firm's team. When putting together a digital ad campaign for them, we looked at past campaigns that featured infographics that illustrated services the company provided. They were well-designed visuals, but not the strongest options, because they didn't communicate the company's biggest differentiator. Instead, we created a campaign that prominently featured the firm's employees: a smiling headshot with a few personal and professional facts that really showcased the people that prospective clients would be working with day-to-day. We wanted to put the visual focus on their strongest asset: the team itself.

No matter which visuals you choose to incorporate in your marketing plan, the production itself is very scalable in terms of skill level and resources available. Nowadays, anyone with an Internet connection can create simple graphics using free, easy-to-use programs such as Canva. Our smartphones have evolved to take incredibly high-quality photos to the point where expensive equipment isn't required to capture the perfect shot. In fact, the *Camera and Imaging Products Association* reported that digital camera sales have dropped as much as 54 percent in recent years (Schneider 2020). Visual content is a powerful marketing tool–and given how simple it is to create high-quality content, there is no need to be afraid of using it.

Video Content

For obvious reasons, 2020 was the year of video. Working from home or using Zoom and webinars became the norm. We were all forced to become more comfortable with video because, for many of us, it suddenly became our second most important form of communication after business e-mail. According to HubSpot's 2020 State of Marketing report, video beat out e-mail marketing, blogging, and infographics as the most used type of marketing content. Suddenly, if you were not doing video, you were not marketing.

There are a number of trends that made this possible. First, we all have video cameras on our laptops and our phones. We use them for personal reasons so we have become more comfortable using them for professional purposes.

Second, we have lowered the professionalism bar for video since we all need to do it every day. We watch a ton of videos from YouTubers and Instagrammers who are doing it themselves. We do not expect polished opening graphics or smooth transitions. Better cameras mean we can get away with lower quality lighting and sound recorded without professional microphones.

Third, social media channels are pushing video. In Facebook's efforts to start streaming live sports and TV events, they prioritized video content to get people used to watching video there. Tik Tok picked up where Vine left off with a much more sophisticated algorithm that created an addictive nature to viewing video on its platform. And YouTube continues to be the world's second largest search engine as well as the dream career path for many preteens, at least the ones in our lives. If another preteen can make $30 million a year on YouTube, you can too.

All companies must have a steady flow of video content produced and promoted in all their marketing channels. Video provides an opportunity to deliver a message with feeling, authenticity, and humanity. Think about the TV or movie stars you watch most frequently. You probably feel like you know them. On a much smaller scale, this is an opportunity video provides for all businesses. It lets your targeted audiences get to know you.

When determining what type of video to create, think carefully about how and where the video will be used. Too often, we've seen full TV commercials make their way onto social media feeds without any edits or adjustments for the new format. Not only is the audience different, but the means of consumption is different.

Let's look at Instagram as an example. This social media platform has three different ways to share video content—we will look at them in more detail as follows. And even if your business doesn't have a presence on Instagram, the questions and process can still be applied as you create your own video content.

Think about your content and the message you're trying to convey. Is the video core to your brand or mission? Is it evergreen—something you would stand by a month, a year, three years from now? Consider investing some more resources into this video so there's higher production quality. In this example, we would post this on our Instagram Grid, or the gallery of posts that lives on your profile page. These posts never disappear (unless you choose to delete them) and should be consistent in voice and tone. We often see these brand videos on YouTube or embedded directly into websites. These videos can accomplish the same type of compelling storytelling that we see with written content.

Perhaps you're trying to capture something in the moment, like a behind-the-scenes video that shows the "making of" your product or service. Maybe you're on-site at a trade show or event and showing off the lay of the land. This content does not need to be as highly produced and, more often than not, it's easier to shoot directly from your phone. Instagram's Stories feature offers an outlet for fast content like this: a place for your in-the-moment video content that disappears within 24 hours. It's perfect for a real-time engagement strategy, and as of 2021, Instagram is reporting that 70 percent of users are viewing this type of video content daily.

There is a hybrid video format, somewhere between the highly produced and the unedited phone footage, which is becoming increasingly popular thanks to TikTok. Phone footage which is edited into quick cuts, produced with sound effects and overlaid text can be found on Instagram's Reels feature. Does your video address a popular trend? Are you positioning yourself as an influencer in your space? This quick, people-focused style of video isn't for everyone, but if you answered yes earlier, it's worth experimenting. There's certainly a lot of growth and opportunity for this emerging type of video.

Audio Content

Audio content is perhaps the most challenging for most companies to understand—until you realize how many people started their own podcast in 2020: Nearly 900,000 new podcasts launched worldwide in 2020, tripling 2019's numbers (Zhorob 2021). Not surprising, because podcasts and audio content in general can be one of the most effective ways to engage with your audience. We have been very lucky to be a guest on podcasts covering everything from the future of trade shows to how to live a good life. Podcasts, whether you participate as a host, cohost, or guest, are powerful because they are based on conversation in a way no other content is. There is the surprise that comes from not really knowing where a conversation will go or what the other people will say. There is an opportunity to really explore a concept, an idea, or a point-of-view through Q&A or the Socratic method. Podcasts have the benefit of not being purely or even mostly promotional because they are about learning from each other and sharing experiences, insights, and thoughts. They are enjoyable and comfortable for many.

If you have a podcast or are thinking about starting one, recognize that they are often only as good as the quality of the host and the guests. As the host, your job is to ask great questions. This requires you to put yourself in the mindset of the listeners, which strategically should be your targeted audience. The benefit of this activity is multifold as entering that mind space will pay off in lots of different ways for the business. Similarly, the guests you choose can benefit the business beyond just making good content. Choose prospects, clients, strategic partners, investors, donors, influencers, and employees who have great stories to tell and with whom you could develop meaningful relationships.

If you are going to pursue a podcast either as a host or guest, be thoughtful about what other types of complementary content can be easily produced. A photo of you and host or guest is great visual content. So is turning a segment of the podcast into a written Q&A for your website. You may even do a video preview of the podcast to help promote it. All of these things are easy to do if you just have a plan and best practices in place.

In general, audio content is a great way to position yourself as a thought leader. Even without pursuing podcasts as a guest or a host, you can record audio reactions to trending topics in your industry or current events that affect your business. Using a tool like Audiogram, this clip can be adapted into video content and shared in an e-mail, sent directly to the media, or posted to social media. If you don't find much time to sit down and create written thought leadership content, this is a quicker way to position yourself as an expert and still share it efficiently with your audiences.

A more unique and often underutilized approach to leveraging audio content would be to connect your organization to music. What does your brand sound like? When someone first calls your business line (or even encounters your website), what sounds—if any—greet them? Some companies have taken this a step further and created branded playlists on platforms like Spotify. It's a bold move to associate your brand with a genre or artist but if it aligns with your mission and message, it could make a powerful impact.

Experiential Content

Experiential content has experienced the biggest transformation of all in 2020, and it will continue to change well into the future. The primary form of experiential content for most companies used to be trade shows and conferences. They provided an opportunity for people to experience products, to listen to talks about new approaches, view poster sessions on new research, or get samples. In April 2020, pretty much all trade shows and conferences were cancelled. Some went online and became virtual events and others were just suspended indefinitely. This put a major wrench in many companies' marketing plans, since a large portion of their budget was invested in these events. It also completely devastated many in the trade show, conference, and events business.

Here at Slice, we host a massive social media conference each year, and prior to 2020, we had hosted hundreds of digital marketing professionals in-person at our annual event. In March of 2020, our plans clearly had to pivot, and we transformed our face-to-face networking event of over 500 attendees into a digital, multitrack experience that still allowed for one-on-one connections. Thanks to online streaming platforms, e-ticketing tools, and communication platforms such as Slack, we pulled it off! Needless to say, we have learned a lot about how experiential content has changed. Following are some tips for those who depend on this type of content.

Before creating a new plan to replace trade shows, you need to ask why you attended trade shows. Some businesses would use trade shows as a way to train or educate their teams, while others would use it for competitive research. However, for most businesses, there are two key reasons that they would attend: to generate new business or to connect with existing customers.

For most business leaders, trade shows were a way to position their brand or product in front of consumers. Salespeople got a chance to shine by directly engaging with potential customers, growing their network of referral sources and partners.

For many business owners and sales teams, joining trade organizations and networking groups was a great way to generate more sales and to increase referral sources.

Trade associations need to retain members for them to continue. This means that they are invested in your success and want to see you thrive. They want to ensure that you will remain a member, see value in your membership, and will refer additional members.

A few ways you can leverage your trade association membership virtually include:

- **Ask for introductions**—One of the simplest things you can do is to ask your member rep if they would introduce you to other members. You're not the only person looking to make new connections during this time and other business leaders will likely be open to connecting and starting the conversation.
- **Contribute content**—Now more than ever, trade associations are looking to amplify the success of their members as a way to get attention. Contact either your member rep or the marketing team for your association and see if they are interested in either collaborating on content or have an option to submit a contributed piece that both your organization and they can amplify.
- **Speak on association panels**—Just because in-person events are off doesn't mean that all events are off. Respondents to a survey by GoodFirms noted a near 75 percent increase in webinars due to COVID-19 (Raymond n.d.). This means that there is a good chance that your trade association is hosting events and, if you express interest, they will be more likely to include your voice in the discussion.

Using the advice previously mentioned, you will likely get some warm introductions or connect with some new people. These introductions and back-and-forth e-mails might mean a meeting, but one meeting does not make a relationship. They might have helped you get your foot in the door, but it is up to you to keep the conversation going and stay top-of-mind. Here's how to follow up with your leads in the virtual space.

The first step of this is to develop a follow-up plan. Specifically, what is your goal for these new contacts? It may differ from person to person; some of these new relationships may be more partner and referral focused instead of directly relating to new business. Others may be sales prospects in the future, but it's not currently the right time.

Here are four tactics you can implement to help stay top-of-mind.

- **Establish a Drip E-Mail Campaign**—One of the simplest things you can do is to add these new contacts to a drip e-mail campaign. This campaign should focus on adding value to your new audience members, such as new blogs, thought leadership, and resources that position your business as a major asset.
- **Connect on LinkedIn**—Ideally, your company should have an active presence on LinkedIn and this was already part of your trade show marketing plan. But in addition to your company page, your sales team should also be active in resharing content and engaging with potential prospects.
- **Market Research**—Surveys are a great way to get to know your audience. Ask your new connections if they would be willing to complete a survey and share more information about themselves, which can allow you to identify trends about your network.
- **Host a Webinar**—Just because events cannot be in person does not mean you cannot host events. Start by identifying potential clients and key referral partners that you want to work with. From there, develop a panel that showcases their expertise, along with yours, and invite them to be one of the panelists. This is a great way to start forming a relationship and generate a warm introduction.

While there are always other things your business can do, these are a few that we have found to be very successful.

However, many business leaders saw the other benefit of trade shows: staying top-of-mind with your current clients and customers. By reconnecting with your existing customers, you have a direct line to people who already know you and are more inclined to either purchase from you again, or to refer you to other people.

In order to best reach your customers, you are going to need some key information about them. While a lot of this information can be found from your general contact lists, such as e-mails and phone numbers, other information may be more niche and will involve more targeted information from relationships that salespeople may have with customers.

- **Their e-mail address**—One of the most important tools for any digital communication. While social media can generate leads and sales, e-mail is still much more effective—especially when you have created a targeted and relevant e-mail list.
- **Have they changed jobs during this?**—During 2020, a lot of people have been forced to change jobs and adjust career paths. Knowing this information will help you target the right people with the right messages.
- **Where can you send mail to them?**—Most people aren't back working from the office yet—and many companies do not plan on giving up remote work any time soon. Direct mail—and even packages—can help your company stand out amongst competitors.

You can collect this information through surveys that are shared through your social media channels and e-mail lists (if you have that data point), or through online forms that gate valuable content or coordinate demo requests. While this may seem like a lot of information to get, it will pay off—especially when you are able to generate sales through a hybrid traditional and digital engagement strategy.

When developing your new engagement strategy, there are two considerations for your plan that shift it away from being a standard trade show marketing plan: It should be multimonth and multitouchpoint.

- **MultiMonth**—When you attend a trade show, you normally
  share that you're attending a few days in advance, you share
  some live footage on social, and then send some follow-up
  e-mails. However, for this type of engagement strategy, you
  can plan for a longer period of time. For example: Social
  media campaigns may not have live trade show footage (or
  the classic booth photo), but now you can share more varied,
  relevant content over a longer period of time. E-mail series do
  not need to last just over the time of the conference—you
  can plan for multiweek e-mail drip campaigns that target
  individuals based on their actions.
- **MultiTouchpoint**—Aside from having a longer time to
  engage contacts, you also now have more ways to engage
  with them. While in-person interactions are often more of a
  comfort zone for salespeople, these engagement strategies can
  incorporate a surround sound approach where you reach your
  targets through a mix of several different channels, including
  virtual events, social media, e-mail marketing, direct mail,
  digital advertising, and more.

Even with trade shows gone, there are still ways to get attention from
existing customers:

- **Webinars**—Even when everyone is working remotely, you
  can still directly engage through webinars. These webinars can
  be structured in any number of ways, including as a standard
  presentation, a roundtable discussion that allows everyone
  to share insights, or a hands-on workshop that guides your
  customers.
- **Share That Tradeshow Swag**—You bought all of that trade
  show swag already, so why not use it? Send it directly to your
  customers to give them a pleasant surprise and a reminder
  that your company is still thinking about them.
- **Virtual Happy Hour or Coffee**—Just because we have to be
  six feet apart does not mean we cannot get drinks. Between

electronic gift cards and services like GoPuff and Gesture, you can easily plan a small happy hour, coffee chat, or even lunch to get some valuable face time with your customers.

Trade shows, conferences, and events are not the only types of experiential content a company can create. There are also virtual games, virtual tours, product configurators, quizzes and tests, certifications, and other ways people can interact and experience your brand–all are various ways to create connected and engaged attention. There is no limit to the creativity you can bring to creating experiences through content.

Just like reevaluating your goals and messaging, businesses should regularly assess content creation as a practice that works for where they are in their strategy. Clients who drag their feet starting a content audit often assume it must be exhaustive. It can start small and grow as you learn what works best for your goals and your team. The largest reason to audit your past content is to avoid repeating the same mistakes and learn where your opportunities could be in near- and long-term planning.

Case Study

One of our clients hired us to develop a series of blog posts but initially did not fully understand our suggestion to include original photography from their representatives on site. It was an added cost, and they felt stock photography captured their work. We explained that although the keywords we established for their campaign were a component of the content, the visual photographs would add another content layer to the work and would attract more users to the website. It was only through a client content audit that we were able to show that over time, the blog posts with original photography had twice as many readers as those using stock photography.

In conclusion, content plays such an important role in harnessing attention that we'd argue you should pause here and really think about your content strategy before continuing on (see Exercises 4.1 and 4.2). Investing time and energy into your communications plan before nailing down these critical building blocks can be futile. Conversely, having a strong handle on your content will set you up for success and make your story memorable and impactful.

Quarterly Content Audit: Quantity

Name of the Piece of Content:

What type of content was it?

Was the content effective?

    1   2   3   4   5

Did it support your goals?

    1   2   3   4   5

Are there opportunities to build on this content?

    1   2   3   4   5

Can you repurpose this content in another way or on another channel?

    1   2   3   4   5

If the total sum above is less than 15: What were some of the challenges you encountered? Why?

Exercise 4.1 Quarterly content creation audit: Quantity

Quarterly Content Audit: Quality

Type of Content:
 Written   Video
 Visual   Experiential
 Audio

Examples of Content:

What was the type of attention desired? Did it earn that attention?

  1   2   3   4   5

What was the type of audience desired? Did it earn that audience?

  1   2   3   4   5

Are there opportunities to build on this content?

  1   2   3   4   5

Can you repurpose this content in another way or on another channel?

  1   2   3   4   5

If the total sum above is less than 15: What were some of the challenges you encountered? Why?

Exercise 4.2 Quarterly content creation audit: Quality

CHAPTER 5

The Four Ways to Bridge Your Content

Moving People Through the Types of Attention to Create Business Growth

The beginning of the book focused on the five types of attention and on learning how to determine what type you need to generate for business growth. In order to move people from one type of attention to the next, you need to present content that is relevant to the type of attention that you are trying to achieve. We call this a **content bridge** because it allows you to move your targeted audience through the different types of attention toward the final type—advocacy.

First Step: Creating Awareness

If you need to generate awareness for your company because not enough people know you exist, you must begin with content that is primarily relevant. It must speak to the audience directly and make it clear why what you do, how you do it, and the reason you do it is important to them. It must communicate that you understand your audience and their challenges and aspirations. At this stage, the goals must be simple because it is the beginning of their journey with you.

We have worked with more than one company that wanted converted attention from their audience but had not built enough awareness of their business. This is an impossible situation for any marketer because the expectations are so out of line with reality. Worse still, many of these clients wanted to talk about their products and services instead of the things that mattered to their targeted audiences.

People tend to appreciate those who help them solve their problems. In his first presidential memoir, Barack Obama writes that the point when things really changed for him came when he was running to be the junior senator from Illinois (Obama 2020). At some point, he stopped talking about his policies and position papers. Instead, he used his stump speeches to repeat what he heard from people on the campaign trail: They were worried they would not be able to retire even after years of working in good jobs. They stayed awake at night concerned that their spouses' cancer treatments would bankrupt them. So instead of talking about his policies, he talked about their worries—and everything changed. He was able to connect—really connect—with them because they felt heard and understood by him. Everyone knows what happened next. He won a seat in the Senate and then had a meteoric rise to the highest office in the United States.

You will know if your content is working—if it is relevant—if people start connecting with you.

First Bridge: Moving From Awareness to Connectedness

Many people think that marketing is all about putting out your message and explaining what your company does. In reality, most businesses find that this approach is ineffective because what your target audience wants to hear, read, or see often isn't what you want to say. Your audience doesn't want to know who you are or what you sell. Instead, they want to hear how you will solve their problems.

When you are trying to move people from being aware of you and your product or service to feeling connected, you must give them a reason why. They need to know how you can better their lives, improve their business, make their kids happier—in short, how you can solve a specific issue for them. You need to explain to them why they need to be connected to you—what your value is to them.

Start by understanding your current customers and clients, as they are the ones who will help your business grow. Do some research and try to understand why they came to you in the first place. What issue are you solving for them? How do you make their lives easier? What do they really think about your product or service?

Depending on your client base, you may be able to do a series of client interviews or conduct a survey. Pay attention to the responses that come up consistently—they will give you a snapshot of what your customers really think of you and your business. Using their feedback, think about how you can make your company, your product, and your service the most relevant it can possibly be to potential new customers.

Case Study

One of our clients is a professional services business-to-business (B2B) company who came to us with the idea of creating a marketing campaign to promote their outsourcing services. This company provided outsourced compliance services for financial companies. It is a niche within a niche within a niche. They were clear on the message they wanted to put out: outsourcing was a great option for businesses. The issue was that this wasn't what their target audience wanted to hear. Instead of hearing about all the benefits of outsourcing, their customers wanted to know that this company would solve a very specific problem: Instead of hiring one person full-time in their company, they could get a whole team of people dedicated to an important part of their business. They wanted to hear that if somebody on that team left, it would not be their responsibility to hire a new person to join the team. They also wanted to hear that they were not going to be a small fish in a big pond—they were going to be important and valued by our client. Finally, they wanted to know that they would be working with a company that was going to grow with them and could handle their increasing complexities as they grew.

It was clear that the message of "outsource, outsource, outsource" would not work. What worked was a message that essentially said: "We would bring a whole team, not just one person." If a staff member left, it would not be a big deal because we will have your back. We have the depth of knowledge to ensure that nothing will be missed.

By switching the message and making it relevant to the target audience, we were able to significantly increase the level of awareness for that client, as well as harness connected attention.

Building real connections with your customers and presenting yourself as a company that understands them is key in moving them from being aware of you to being truly connected. Similar to building relationships in your personal life, the people who really get you are often the same people who seem to naturally understand what is important to you. Show your customers that you care about the same issues, and your relationship with them will grow stronger.

So how do you create a message that proves to your customers that you both share common interests and values?

Put yourself in the shoes of your best complete customers. What is keeping them up at night? What are their most pressing problems? Once you understand that, you will have the beginning of your strategy for relevant content that connects with your audience.

Second Bridge: Moving From Connected Attention to Engaged Attention

As we know, connected attention is where your customers simply want to hear more while engaged attention is where you begin to have a two-way conversation. People are much more likely to have a two-way conversation with you if they believe that they will get value out of that conversation and that talking to you will make their lives better or solve a problem they have. Think about the people who have added the most value in your life, impacted your business, and changed your way of thinking. That change, that new perspective is what matters when moving your audience to engaged attention.

While that might seem really obvious in professional services, it might be really difficult to make your clients see that in product sales where you have to challenge existing assumptions. That is because when you think about a product that you really love, it is usually a product that is designed in a way that is incredibly researched and thought-out. The process and research that went into designing or creating the product are all based on insights—insights generated by research, development, and testing. Once you have conducted your research and done your own testing and development, you can use those insights to kick start that two-way conversation with your audience.

Third Bridge: Moving From Engaged Attention to Converted Attention

The next bridge helps us move people from giving our clients engaged attention to converted attention. The goal here is to develop content for them that is actionable. The messaging should be very clear and ask such questions as what steps they should take next, what conversations they should have, what approaches they should change, what best practices they should put in place, what people they should hire, which products they should buy, and which companies they should consult with. Using those prompts can help you create action-oriented content to get people to buy in. If we move outside your target audience, which is the customer or client, and instead think about employees as an audience, again, you want to give them something actionable because that is what will make them want to come work for you. When you say: "Here is how you can make a difference. Here is how you can live your values. Here is how you can work with people that you love to work with. Here is how you can be excited about getting up every morning to do the work that you are going to do," these are the kinds of messages that get people to want to join your company. We can also take the case of investors or donors. When we give them actionable content, it's something like: "Here is how putting your money to work with us is going to make a difference, or achieve your goals of getting that money back, or make an impact on the community, or support a cause that you really care about, or find a cure." All of these messages are action-oriented, helping move your audience from engaged to converted.

Fourth Bridge: Moving From Converted Attention to Advocacy

The last bridge moves people from converted attention to becoming advocates through inspiring content. Advocates are people who use the attention that they are getting in order to get attention for you. It is a generous action. Yes, sometimes advocates get paid and can act out of self-interest, but ultimately, what they are doing is helping to make your business succeed. To create your own advocates, start with your own employees, as they make the best advocates, whether it be for your company, philanthropic goals, or for your products and services. Approach those employees who you think would make great advocates and explain that as you are looking to launch your product or service, you would like to lean on their expertise to help you craft the message that speaks to your audience. Tell them that you have noticed that they are interested in similar things as your target audience, that perhaps they go to the same conferences or read the same publications, and that you want to position them as a thought leader on this new product or service and to support their opportunities for professional growth within your industry. That you want to submit them for speaking opportunities, byline articles on your behalf, and feature them in a video about your product or service.

Think about how inspiring that conversation would be! When you empower somebody by offering to support them, provide new opportunities and help them to be recognized at a whole different professional level, it encourages positive advocacy on behalf of your company.

Another great way to inspire people to become advocates is to engage the people who refer business to you, also called centers of influence. Very often, they make great advocates. The conversation you might want to have with them is to make them feel that they are on the inside. For example, if you are going to be hosting a new event, encourage them to be part of the host committee. Other ways to make them feel that they are on the inside could be encouraging them to speak on a webinar or co-write a byline article with you. In doing so, these centers of influence will be promoting both themselves and your company to their community members. It's a win-win for everyone.

The most important thing to remember about advocate attention is that it feeds the other types of attention, as well as generating more advocate attention. When you start to highlight and cocreate content with centers of influence, others will want to join in. By setting this example, you are inspiring additional advocates to come to you, and that, again, can be very powerful. When you are showcasing your advocate attention to people who are considering converting, very often, the power of advocacy will push them over the finish line. It will give them the trust and certainty to buy from you and will help address any fears.

It is important to remember to engage with your advocate attention. Inspiring content is example-based. Start by identifying your centers of influence and have a conversation on how to make them feel part of the team. Once you get a groove going, new advocates will want to join too.

Now that you understand the bridges and the changes in audience behavior, you might ask yourself: "How do I decide what I need to do at this point?" To answer that question, you need to identify which of the bridges to focus on and what type of content best supports that message. For instance, video or experiential content resonates the best with inspiring content. In order to convey something in a truly inspiring way, it needs to be emotional, and emotions are best communicated in video or in-person. Being able to see somebody's facial expressions and hear their voice and tone is very powerful.

Audio or written content is great when you need the space to fully articulate your message—this works well for insightful content. If your content is data-driven, infographics or charts are another interesting way to convey your message. Actionable content is best served as written content because it has to tell people what the steps are. You can also use video content, such as an explainer video or a product or service demo. Relevant content needs to get people's attention right away and be easy to digest. That's why visual content is your best bet. The adage "a picture is worth a thousand words" is exactly what you want to achieve through compelling visual content.

Types of Attention: Engaged Attention

At some point, you've probably been to a party where you got stuck in a corner talking to someone who wouldn't let you get a word in. We've all had a conversation where the other person talked about themselves the whole time and never stopped rattling on to listen to anyone else. Let's change that scenario and imagine that someone at that party did want to know about you, to understand you, to know what you cared about, and what you were interested in. Imagine that this person then provided some really interesting new information about something that really mattered to you. You left the party feeling excited and you would probably want to stay in touch with this new friend, and to keep your conversation going. That is an example of how you move people from being connected with you to being engaged. This engaged attention is obtained through insight.

In the same way, you have more insight on what you do and the products and services you offer than any of your audiences. Most people don't really have the time, knowledge, or expertise to go as deep into your subject area as you can—they simply cannot invest in it the way that you do. If someone does invest in your field, they get to know it and understand it in a totally new and different way—a way that adds a lot of value to them and causes them to want to be engaged with you.

For instance, let's say that you are an expert in widget making and you know more about what you are making than anyone else. Your audience is concerned about your supply chain, fearing that there will not be enough materials available for them to make sure that they can obtain the widgets that they need. But you spend a lot of time in supply chain and you know that if you get certain items from country A versus country B, you will be able to get them more quickly in case there is going to be a shortage of component applications. You are working really hard to replace those components and know that there is going to be a decrease in demand coming up. You have all of this information, all of this insight, and if you want to, you could actually provide some concrete evidence, data, and perspective to your audience that they can't, or don't have the time or money to get, on their own. You know significantly more than they do, because if you don't, chances are they are not going to want to work with you anyway.

So how can you share that information on an ongoing basis? Think about how you can take these insights and incorporate them into your five types of content. How can you showcase your expertise in a totally new and different way that no one else is doing?

Many years ago, we worked with students at the Wharton School at the University of Pennsylvania. Our company, Slice Communications, is a woman-owned business, and we get to know a lot of other women-owned businesses. We work in marketing and communications so whenever we talk to other women-owned businesses we ask them about their plans with marketing and what is working and not working for them as women in business. One thing that we see consistently is that there is often a lack of in-depth knowledge when it comes to social media. As we worked with the students at Wharton to complete a research program together, we selected a random sample of women-owned businesses and looked at whether they had social media channels such as LinkedIn, Facebook, Instagram, or Twitter and if they did, whether they were active or inactive. What were they doing on their channels? Were they using them in the way that the most sophisticated marketers, or even the best small business marketers, were using them? Again and again, we found that they weren't. After a year, we published this research and included insights into where these women-owned businesses were falling short compared to other small businesses and medium-sized businesses. We fed back the insights we got from our research to the businesses. Once the study was published, we did a series of talks that were presented at the National Women's Business Enterprise National Council's (WBENC) conference and turned out to be one of the most highly rated presentations at the conference that year. Cass was honored to be recognized by WBENC as a rising star woman business owner under the age of 40. Because of this work and its contribution to this community, it ended up being a great opportunity for us to help develop a lot of new relationships, many of which led to getting new business. Most importantly, it raised our brand and company profile within WBENC and positioned us as a company that cares and is willing to give back to the community and that has valuable information to share. As a result of this study, we closed a huge account with a global fortune 500 company even though we had not set out to do that when we had first begun the project. It was a great result of being seen and positioned as somebody who has insights to share.

Types of Attention: Actionable Content

Most people like to be told what to do. Of course, very few people actually admit this as they like to think that they are independent and they have their own mind about things. Naturally, that is the case in some situations, but a majority of people just want to be told what decision to make because it makes their lives easier. That is where actionable content comes in. If you tell people what actions to take, you are much more likely to get them to take those actions.

There are three different types of actionable content you can take. The first is a simple and direct "what to do" type of action. Examples of this actionable content are "click here," "buy this now," "sign up in advance," or "get your ticket." All of those are WHAT actions. If you have a more complicated sales process, you might need to communicate that WHAT action a little differently. The messaging could be "sign up to chat with us," or "come visit us at our booth." The WHAT actions are the ones that create business, moving people from engaged to converted. Of course, the tone has to be right—you can't just order your audience around. You need to communicate in a way that sounds like them, is clear and consistent, and give the WHAT action again and again in different ways.

The HOW action is suitable for complex decisions that are involved in buying a service. If you tell your audience how to do something and they realize they do not have the capacity or expertise to actually follow through on that HOW, they will come to you for help as you are perfectly placed to do that. The HOW actions can be communicated as, for example, here are "the five steps," "the six new approaches," or "the how to." These HOW conversations will lead to WHAT conversations, but in a very different way.

The third type of actionable content is the WHY action: Here is why you should do this. There are a lot of good books, for example those by Simon Sinek, that can help you start the WHY conversation both internally and externally. Communicating the WHY can often be the most complex of the actions because it requires the most research and analysis. We talked earlier about messaging and mentioned that your point of view should be used here in the WHY action. WHY actions often require more emotion as you communicate them and are often best communicated on video where people can see facial expressions, hear tone of voice, and understand the concern or excitement that comes with the WHY.

Remember, if you do not first build a foundation of relevance and insight, getting to actionable content will be really hard. People often skip this type of content entirely because they are afraid of sounding as if they are telling others what to do. This is where tone and voice are so important. You need to position yourself as just trying to be helpful in providing tips, guidance, and assistance—this makes a huge difference in the way this content is received and whether or not people take the action.

Whatever the action you are using, it has to be simple and it has to be possible. One of our client's WHAT actions was for people to download a particular white paper. They were promoting it primarily through social media, and if you know social media, you know that it is predominantly mobile and continues to be mobile. The problem was that in order to download the white paper, you had to go to their website and the mobile experience on the website was horrible. It asked customers to fill out their information before receiving any content, showed them a very long legal disclaimer that users had to scroll through, and after all of that scrolling, when users eventually got to the contact form, it asked for about 14 different types of information to be completed on a mobile device. It's not a surprise that nobody wanted to do that. No one wanted to go through that poor user experience. The lesson: If you are asking for an action, make it easy to do. Otherwise, you are never going to get people to take that action.

Another one of our clients, a magazine publisher, wanted to create an action for their sponsors. They wanted to obtain user generated content by having their magazine followers on social media provide them with a photo. In return for this photo, a tree would be planted. For many people, that is not a good trade off of value if you have to go and take a picture, give the company your e-mail address and all of your contact information and in exchange, you may get a tree planted on your behalf somewhere. You may not even know where. The magazine publisher was not able to convert users, followers, and people in this campaign. It's important to think about the value exchange of the actions that you are asking and make sure it makes sense and is easy to do.

Types of Attention: Advocate Attention

The wonderful thing about advocate attention is that it feeds the other types of attention. When you have your advocates out there using their attention to help you, it increases your brand awareness and gets more people to be willing to connect with you. It encourages more people to engage and start that two-way conversation with you. Finally, it can help people convert to becoming your clients, customers, investors, donors, or employees. That is because hearing from a third party, not you but other people, can often be the most compelling thing that moves people through the five types of attention. So how do you get advocates to help you generate advocate attention?

Let's first recognize that having advocates and getting advocate attention are two totally separate things. There may be people who love you, your company, and your product and service. When asked, they may be your reference and speak positively about you. While it is wonderful to have those sorts of advocates, it is unlikely that they will help generate attention for you or that they will be active and proactive in using the attention that they are getting to help you grow unless you put a concerted plan in place. The way to move people from converted to advocate is to do something inspiring. It is about providing inspiring content, of which there are several types.

The first way to inspire people is to educate them by providing information, tips, best practices, or training on how to generate attention for themselves and for you. Educational content can come in a variety of forms. For instance, you may want to do some training for your customers. Personal branding training is a good place to start so they understand how to build their own personal brand and how to increase their networks via networking training. This is all incredibly valuable. Or you may want to organize a course on providing content. You can reach out and ask them to be part of a webinar or ask them for a quote that you could include in written material. You could even ask them to take a picture of themselves that you could incorporate into your visual content. All of this education and support is away to inspire and help them help you.

The second type of inspiring content is really what we call "the greater good" inspiring content. This type of content is the kind that can benefit both your and your clients' companies or brands. Companies and individuals don't always understand this concept, so you may need to show them examples of what it might look like to work together, demonstrate how they would benefit and how it can grow their business to help them achieve their goals and aspirations. This will help your audience see the bigger picture and grasp the bigger impact that can be made when you team up. All of that is incredibly powerful.

The third type of inspiring content is your own content. This content needs to be entertaining and make your audience want to share it with others. This is powerful because when you entertain your audience, you entertain your advocates. It really is as easy as it sounds. People want that opportunity, even if you are in a B2B space. So whether you are a B2B or B2C company or nonprofit, if you can create something that is funny and makes your audience feel good, that entertaining content can go a very long way. It is often the hardest to do, but it yields incredible value. That entertainment content can often be the most valuable for advocates to use. Some advocates will develop their own entertaining content and some will do it together with you. In sharing it together, you can get more value for them and for you. When you think about inspiring content, consider all three parts: educational inspiring content, bigger picture (greater good) inspiring content, and entertainment inspiring content.

Inspiring content is the most difficult type of content to create and that is because it really does require emotional investment. Think about the emotion that you want to create. Do you want people to be surprised? Do you want them to be excited? Do you want them to feel like they are part of something? Do you want them to feel included? Do you want them to feel silly? Do you want them to feel energized? Identify the emotion and you will be much more likely to connect with your audience.

It's a good idea to bring a creative on board to help you craft your inspiring content–an outsider will often have a fresh and exciting perspective that can help you reach a wider audience.

One of the companies we worked with worked in consumer products, creating powders for diaper rash and chafing. They identified a potential advocate, a semiprofessional wrestler who really loved their product. The issue was that there weren't many opportunities for this potential advocate to really generate a whole lot of attention for our client. So, we identified an opportunity: the Swamp Ass Prevention Day. Believe it or not, that is a day that actually exists. We reached out to this person who is known for being entertaining, and said, "Hey, if we do this thing together, it could benefit you and it could benefit us. You can get a lot of views, you could have something funny to talk about, you can add something to your feed, and we will give you some free products." He agreed. This gave our client a fantastic number of views, way more reach, and great feedback from their customers. It also gave them something to do for Swamp Ass Prevention Day. Our client's company became relevant to people who cared about Swamp Ass as a professional day. The wrestler made a video and it was hilarious. We gave him creative freedom since he was outside of the organization, to really do what he wanted and needed to do, and the result was tremendous. It helped the brand get a whole lot of advocate attention and really put them on the map to help them compete for Swamp Ass Prevention Day.

Inspiring content is the most challenging type of content. You must think about turning your converted audience into your advocate audience. We also recommend a totally separate marketing communications plan, one that is not focused on customers, clients, or any of the other types of audience per se, but one that is solely focused on advocates, on giving them education, the bigger picture, and providing support for their creativity to create entertainment. It makes sense that somebody within your organization really owns the advocate communications plan in and of itself, separate but supportive of the overall marketing plan.

CHAPTER 6

The Power of Surround Sound

Why One Touchpoint Will Never Be Enough

Imagine you pick up the newspaper or turn on the TV, and you see a great story about a company or nonprofit organization. Then you see something about that same organization on your Facebook, Twitter, or LinkedIn feed. Then you get an e-mail about a special event or a new product that the company is offering. You may not have paid attention to the first story you saw, but by the time you see the same brand mentioned several times, you will start to take notice. That is the power of the surround sound. It is the Holy Grail of attention marketing because it works so well.

Surround sound is effective for creating awareness, but it works far beyond that by creating five types of attention, starting with connected attention. People who want to connect with you want to hear from you in many different ways, not just one. Engaged attention will often follow when people have regular, ongoing opportunities for conversations with you. Converted attention comes much more quickly when there is a concerted effort aimed at giving people lots of different reasons to apply, buy, or join. And there is nothing like surround sound to give advocates opportunities to share and promote.

Implementing a surround sound approach and making it the center of your marketing effort is no different than the Flywheel concept the great Jim Collins outlines in *Good to Great: Why Some Companies Make the Leap and Others Don't* (2001). A flywheel is a large, heavy wheel on an axel. It can be incredibly powerful if only you can get it moving. The trick is that once you get it to start moving, it is really easy to keep it moving. As Collins writes, "Each turn of the flywheel builds upon work done earlier, compounding your investment of effort.... The huge heavy disk flies forward, with almost unstoppable momentum."

That is the same power we see in surround sound. It can be hard to get started, but it must be done in order to get the momentum needed for people to start hearing and seeing your brand constantly and in a way that cannot be ignored.

In our experience, there are three marketing communications tactics that are the most effective and efficient for organizations that want to create surround sound because they build on each other: PR, social media, and e-mail marketing. Together, they get the flywheel of attention going with momentum that delivers return on investment.

So, who in your organization pushes the flywheel? The marketing team, of course. But it will move much more quickly and easily if others help. There are two types of people in your organization who are best suited to this job: thought leaders and employee champions.

"Thought leadership" as a term can seem very jargony, so let me make it simple: Thought leaders are the people in your organization who have the best ideas. Their ideas can be about innovative products, human behavior, science, technology, new approaches to old problems, new problems, how your industry is changing, new opportunities, the list goes on. They are thoughtful AND they can articulate their thoughts. They want to have a voice. They want to share what they are thinking, learning, and questioning. When they are involved as media spokespeople, social media influencers, and content producers, everything moves more easily. Thought leaders often just need structure and support to get their ideas out to others.

Employee champions are those employees who are so engaged and love their work so much that they want to tell other people about it. They live your values, believe in your vision, and find any way they can to contribute to the success of your organization. Often, they are not marketing people. They may or may not have natural communication skills. But they have passion—passion that can go away if it is not nurtured. They want to speak on your behalf, they just don't know how.

These people need to be identified and trained. Professional development and learning how to use marketing communications channels will go a long way toward getting them pushing the flywheel and creating surround sound.

The rest of this chapter is devoted to exploring some new ways to use PR, social media, and e-mail marketing in detail. We have found that a military analogy works best when explaining how PR, social media, and e-mail marketing work together. Think about PR as the air cover. It can cover a lot of ground and create a lot of attention. It is often expensive and hard to pull off since most people have no idea how to do it, just like flying a plane. Social media is your ground troops. Every day, it goes to work making progress, moving forward, creating more attention incrementally. E-mail marketing is your sharpshooter. When used well, it directs the right message to the right individual or segmented group at the right time. Together, they create a force that is strong and dynamic.

Of course, there are many different approaches to how to execute PR, social media, and e-mail marketing, but these are ours and we are confident that they will help you.

Public Relations

"Public relations" is an unfortunate term, because it is neither intuitive nor communicative. It can mean anything. Ivy Lee, largely recognized as the founder of PR due to the work he did turning around the Rockerfeller name, is quoted as saying, "I have never been able to find a satisfactory phrase to describe what I do" (quoted in Cutlip 2013, 126). The Wikipedia entry for PR takes it a step further in its entry with this statement: "In 1948, historian Eric Goldman noted that the definition of public relations in Webster's would be 'disputed by both practitioners and critics in the field'" (Wikipedia n.d.).

Yup, sounds about right. Dana has always said that she has been working in PR for 20 years, and her parents still have no idea what she does. So, we are going to try to make it simple. PR is about getting earned media coverage, speaking opportunities, and recognition through awards. Sure, there could be other parts to it, but for most organizations, focusing on these three areas will go a long way.

Media Relations

Let's begin with earned media coverage. There are four ways most organizations can generate media coverage:

1. **News Releases**—Press releases are what most people think about when they think of PR. Press releases are best used for hard news: a new product, service, partnership, building, leader, and so on. They are not useful in generating media coverage for thought leadership. A new website or blog, a speaking opportunity, a video series, and so on are not newsworthy. They may be interesting, but they won't convince an editor to include you in an article.

2. **Editorial Briefings**—This is an opportunity to sit down with a reporter, either in person or over the phone, and share your background, areas of expertise, and what value you can add to the publication. These conversations should not be about your products and services. Instead, you should talk about some of the topics around which you have created content. Share your ideas, your experience, the concerns you're hearing from people in the industry, and your point of view. Let them know who you are and how you can help them now or in the future.

3. **Pitching**—This is the most effective form of media outreach for thought leaders. It can be time-consuming and requires consistency. Each piece of content you develop is based on an idea, and that idea can be pitched to reporters or editors for them to write about or cover. A pitch is typically an e-mail that explains the idea, why it matters to their audiences, and your perspective on it. Some reporters will bite right away. Others may need to hear from you a few times before responding. Either way, it's a numbers game. But there's a big trophy in the form of a lot of views if you are willing to play ball or pay someone to do it for you.

4. **Newsjacking**—There are a lot of things happening in the world every day and a lot of news being covered. Chances are that you, as a thought leader, have a perspective on some of those things. Newsjacking is a PR technique where you listen for relevant things happening in the news and then reach out to reporters offering yourself

as an expert on the topic for additional stories. It can be incredibly effective and catapult a thought leader to the national stage. It too, takes time, as well as an awareness of what's happening in the world.

There are two primary types of earned media interactions that will lead to coverage. Sometimes, reporters report stories. They identify a subject, interview people on the topic, do research, and draft an article or broadcast piece. These are usually news stories, human interest pieces, or profiles. Sometimes they are also case studies or trend pieces. The pros of getting media coverage via an interview include the credibility of being in a reported story, the inclusion of other thought leaders, and the limit on how much work you need to do as the source or spokesperson. The major con is that you cannot control the story or how you are included in it. Of course, if something is factually incorrect, you may be able to get it changed, but you really have no recourse if a reporter doesn't want to make a change.

Bylined Articles

Another name for contributed content is bylined article. Since many media outlets, particularly those in trades, have shrinking budgets to pay for reporters, they are more open than ever to taking content you develop. Often, they will have editorial guidelines that you need to follow and deadlines that you need to hit. Most will require original content, meaning something that hasn't been published elsewhere on the Internet or in print. That said, you will usually have complete control of what is published as long as you follow the guidelines and don't promote yourself, your products, or your services.

While your company will have a lot of control over a bylined article placement because you write it, getting your message across in an interview with a reporter is much more difficult. That is because a conversation with a reporter is unlike any other conversation you will ever have. Your job in the Q&A is not to answer questions. Your job is to deliver messages. There has been much written on media training and preparing for a media interview, so if you find yourself in the spokesperson seat, do not be afraid to ask for help. It is like anything else—becoming a good spokesperson requires practice.

Speaking Opportunities

Conferences and trade shows—in-person or virtual—are major drivers of many industries. They are opportunities for people to network and learn. Organizers (and Dana is one of them for a few different business groups and nonprofits) are always looking for speakers. We want someone with something new to say, and we want to make sure they say it with the right kind of energy. A great speaker can change a conference, a way of doing business, or even set their own organization on a new path for growth.

Getting speaking opportunities can be challenging, so here are some tips:

- **Start Small**—We cannot tell you how many times giving a talk at a small, local or regional chapter of a trade association has led to bigger opportunities for our clients and us. That is because organizations with local chapters talk with each other. They compare notes on great speakers and exchange contact information. Dana personally participated in a panel in front of a group of no more than 25 participants. It was well received and within a year, she was one of the most highly rated speakers at the national conference. Small speaking opportunities are simply auditions for big speaking opportunities and should be treated as such. If you are on the marketing team, get your thought leaders in this mindset. If you are a spokesperson who really wants to grow your presence, understand you will have to spend time in the minors.
- **Make Videos and Publish Content**—How do you know someone is smart and interesting enough to engage an audience? Their videos are always a good place to start. That means that as a marketing person, you are going to be much more effective pitching a talk for one of your thought leaders if you can show the selection committee that person's energy and personality. Make original videos, record speaking

opportunities, set up webinars on your own. Publishing regular written content is another way to showcase that your thought leader has a lot to say on a topic that matters to people. A regular column on Medium or LinkedIn Pulse, a white paper, or even a book, will be proof that you are proposing a high-quality speaker who will enhance the conference.

- **Grow a Following**—The other way to prove that a speaker is worth inviting is to demonstrate that people listen to them. Speakers with lots of LinkedIn connections or Twitter followers obviously have credibility and popularity. They can invite their followers to come to the event or buy a ticket. For that reason, work with your thought leaders to grow their social media presence and following. Make sure they know why and the benefit it will bring to them and the company. This takes time, but it really supports the flywheel once it gets going.

- **Network**—The last way you are likely to get a speaking opportunity is to respond to a call for speakers. Sure, you may get lucky, but it is a lot of work to craft a speaking submission and not get the call. That said, the people who make the decisions are just people. Regular people. They are often easy to find online and anyone can get to know them. Consider it part of your plan throughout the year. Try to meet them in person at the show or conference. Connect with them on LinkedIn. At the end of each conference or event, ask them what they heard about the speakers and who was the most well-received. All of this will help you get the best speaking opportunities.

Awards and Recognition

Most awards today are pay-to-play. They make money for the trade association, groups, or media organizations that make the awards. They get application fees, ticket fees, and sometimes even revenue from plaques, banners, or stickers formalizing the awards. That is okay. It just means that awards, if they are part of your plan, need to be part of your budget.

The most important thing to recognize is that awards have value, but you have to create that value. They can make employee champions feel pride, customers feel confidence, centers of influence feel respect, and competitors feel jealous. Applying for awards takes time, and you may have to do it a few times before you win. But once you do, share your win every opportunity you have.

Social Media

Social media has become a primary tool for brands and companies to talk to their customers directly. Here are some strategies that we use at Slice to ensure that social media contributes to creating surround sound.

Building a Following:

We are often asked which social networks make the most sense for businesses. The answer is, "it depends." Social platforms are actively changing each day, meaning recommendations and best practices evolve at that same pace. But it's safe to say, if you are just starting to build a following on social media, you should only invest in one or two channels. Do not try to do them all. You will end up overextending yourself and doing nothing.

Determining where your audience is will help you determine which one or two social channels you should invest your time in. Talk to a few people that represent your potential audience. Ask them where they get news and information. Knowing the pace at which these platforms adapt, you can use this cheat sheet as a basic guide:

> **LinkedIn**—Business-to-business professionals are here, particularly those in professional services. Yes, many people use LinkedIn to look for jobs or recruit more employees. But many other people use LinkedIn to research products and services, companies, and leaders before they make a decision to buy. Since being bought by Microsoft, LinkedIn's newsfeed has dramatically evolved. More and more people are going there for business-focused news, events, and insights. It can be easy, though time consuming, to build an online network and following.
>
> **Twitter**—This is a must-do if you're in politics, news commentary, or technology. It's also the easiest way to connect with people if you do a lot of speaking at conferences. People

can easily find you, mention you, post photos of you, and ask you questions. All serious speakers should have a Twitter promotional plan. Building a following here is also easy, but time consuming.

Facebook—Facebook now boasts more than 2.8 billion monthly users worldwide, with nearly 70 percent of all adults reporting regular use of the platform. We've seen it work for thought leaders in most industries, not just consumers or non-profits. There are some choices to be made if you're going to set up a Facebook presence as a thought leader: whether to use a personal, business, or public persona page. This is one where you should probably consult a digital marketing professional to help you set it up. The fastest way to develop a following is through paid ads, so make sure you incorporate a budget into your planning.

Instagram—Instagram is a photo and video content platform. Reading long-form content, such as articles or blog posts, really isn't a thing that happens there. But thought leaders on lifestyle, real estate, design, and other visual industries can have success on Instagram. So can speakers and authors, as long as they invest in high-quality photos for the platform. If Instagram is right for you, also plan for a budget. Since it's owned by Facebook, Instagram also works best when you're buying ads.

Posting

Your posting strategy—what, how often, and so on—depends on the social media platform you've chosen. Here are some general guidelines:

LinkedIn—Post three to four times a week. Include at least one post with a piece of content you've written yourself. Include one post about third-party content you find interesting, and mention why you think it's interesting. The other two posts may be about an event you will be attending or have attended, news from your company, news from a trade association or nonprofit you support, a shared post from a colleague, a congratulatory post for a client or customer, or something else.

Twitter—Post as needed. Whenever you have new content to share, do it on Twitter. When attending or speaking at events, ramp up your posts right before a conference or speaking opportunity, be very active during the event, and be sure to share information after the fact.

Facebook—Be sure to post three to four times per week. Consider the audience and the platform when posting. Yes, it's ok to post about your content. It's also cool to post about your business and speaking gigs. Don't post personal items unless you're okay with your business community seeing them. Keep it light and know that people may be looking at your posts while they're waiting in line or sitting on the toilet.

Instagram—It's okay to limit Instagram posts to twice per week for most thought leaders. The exception is if you are a professional influencer, and your job is to post to Instagram. Remember, Instagram is for sharing visual content. Unless you're spending money on ads, you can't link to articles or longer-form pieces you've written. Therefore, if traffic to a website is your goal, this platform is unlikely to drive any until you start spending money on advertising.

There are also some best practices you can use regardless of the social media channel:

- **Never Once**—It is a mistake to post a piece of content just once and think all the people you want to see it will see it. They won't. Don't post the same thing over and over, though. Your timeline will look completely insane. Instead, pick apart your content and find a few interesting ways to get people's attention with it.
- **Always with a Link and/or Hashtag**—Every post on every platform should include a link and, if applicable, at least one hashtag. The exception is links on Instagram, as mentioned, unless you are using third-party tools like Linktree. Hashtags

are important because they help people find posts on topics that interest them. That's why you must do research into hashtags people use. When you use them, you increase the likelihood of people finding your content because they're interested in the topic. Similarly, be sure you include a link so there is a call-to-action. Ideally, use a tagged link (and visit www.SliceCommunications.com to learn how to do that) so you can track where traffic originated.

- **Sometimes with an Image**—Sometimes, a link you include in a social post will automatically generate an image. That's great! As long as it's a relevant, on-brand image. If no image populates, you will often have the opportunity to add one. Whatever you do, don't miss the opportunity to include an image when you can. A picture is worth a thousand words, as they say. That's particularly true when characters are being counted.

- **Usually with a Mention**—Other people matter. They help you with your business, they give you good ideas, they connect you with even more people, and they have people that follow them. When possible, @mention them in your posts. Or @mention their companies. Either way, you will get the attention of others and the people that follow them.

Interacting

Social media should never be a one-way street. You cannot just post and think that suddenly people are going to start following you because you're brilliant. Be sure to interact with everyone mentioning you. They are trying to start a conversation, so join them. Find others that you care about and start conversations with them. You'll likely find some great collaborators and maybe even a few clients or employees.

E-Mail Marketing

We love e-mail marketing and will fight anyone who says it is dying. Think about it: How much time have you spent on your e-mail today?

This week? This month? This year? We love it. We are addicted to it. We are never letting it go. And believe it or not, we want to get e-mail messages, even from companies.

In our experience, there are three important roles that good e-mail marketing can (and should) play in your marketing communications strategy: top-of-mind, event attendance, and online sales. This is because we are trained to act based on an e-mail more than we are trained to act based on any other marketing communication.

- **Top-of-Mind**—There is so much information clutter in the world today that many people have a hard time remembering everything; companies that depend on referral and word-of-mouth marketing do better when they're regularly reminding their targeted audiences how they can help (without being annoying, of course).
- **Event Attendance**—While social media and PR are great for letting people know about an upcoming event or conference, e-mail is what actually drives signups, ticket sales, attendance, and engagement.
- **Online Sales**—Over and over again, we've seen there's nothing better for e-commerce sales than e-mail marketing. Sure, social media can and should drive a lot of traffic but e-mail often closes the deal.

A great e-mail marketing program really comes down to four things. They are all pretty simple but each of them takes regular time and effort. This is not a "set it and forget it" method. Sending an e-mail can be a superpower if it is done correctly. But with great power comes great responsibility.

Building and Segmenting a List

There are people who want to get e-mails from you. Some admit it openly and some do not, but they want it regardless. Who are those people for your business? Customers? Employees? Partners? Centers of influence? Suppliers? Industry leaders? Employee applicants? Your former colleagues and friends? You need this list. It will change your life and your business.

More importantly, you need this list in a software designed for e-mail marketing. It cannot just sit in your CEO's Outlook, an Excel file, or a Customer Relationship Management (CRM) application. It is useless unless it is in a place where you can separate contacts based on industry, audience type, and behavior.

Maybe you do not have a list. Our team at Slice put together this nifty list of ideas of how you can start building it:

- E-Mail Marketing 101: Make It Easy to Sign Up On Your Website
  - o Add a simple e-mail subscription box in the footer of all your web pages.
  - o Create a popup on your website that encourages visitors to subscribe.
  - o Have your employees add a newsletter opt-in to their e-mail signature.
- Use Your Content: Ways to Leverage Content to Capture E-Mails
  - o Gate any longer form—or more valuable—content on your website, so visitors must at least submit an e-mail address to get access. This could include:
    - Whitepapers and eBooks
    - Checklists and Templates
    - Prerecorded Videos and Online Courses
  - o Start a blog on your website, and encourage visitors to sign up for new updates.
  - o Leverage SEO best practices to optimize your website for organic traffic.
  - o Host a live webinar event or panel, with an e-mail opt-in to register.
- Reach Subscribers Off Your Website: Leveraging Social Media
  - o Promote your website and original content across your social media channels.
  - o Ask your followers and their network to share your content further.

- o Link your sign-up forms on your social platforms, and post about them organically.
- o Run a paid lead generation ad on social media, leveraging original content or news.
- o Host a giveaway or contest that users sign up for by submitting their contact information.

Your e-mail list is one of your most important marketing assets. There is so much potential revenue in those contacts, it should be treated like gold. That means it needs to be cleaned. Old contacts, irrelevant ones, ones that never interacted with you at all, need to be removed. Your most critical contacts who have changed jobs and have new e-mail addresses need to be updated. And your newest, most powerful contacts need to be added every month at the very least.

E-Mail Broadcasts

E-mail broadcasts, that is newsletters, play an important role for most companies. They are a one-to-many communication that keeps an organization top of mind. They keep the flywheel spinning. There are probably exciting things happening with and around your company that people on your e-mail list want to know. This is different from things you want to say, so just keep that in mind as you plan out the content that goes into your newsletter. They may want to know about job openings at the company, awards or new contracts you have received, or work you are doing in the community. All of these things will either make them feel good about already working with you or possibly even convince them that you are the type of company that they would like to work with. Most often, the type of attention e-mail newsletters encourage is brand awareness. Occasionally, they can help with converted attention or even engaged attention, but awareness is the primary result most of the time.

There are other types of e-mail broadcasts that can be used to promote very specific types of content. E-mail is still the primary driver of event sales and registrations. It can also rival social media posts and ads for directing content downloads. The thing about these types of e-mails is that you cannot just send one. For events, we have found six e-mails to be about the right number for smaller events and webinars. For large events and conferences, the number is much higher. There are a lot of reasons for this, including how and when people access their e-mail, how you can overcome their procrastination, and how they make decisions to attend events. Regardless, the number of e-mails you send to get converted attention on content is high. Do not let the fear of people unsubscribing prevent you from doing what it takes to get the attention of those most likely to engage and convert.

That said, you do not want to spin the e-mail flywheel so fast that it flies off and stops completely. Do some research into your audience and their behavior, and you will easily find the right cadence for sending newsletters and broadcasts. If you have an established relationship with an ideal client, consider asking them for their own opinions and habits in regard to e-mail. If this anecdotal evidence reveals common pain points (such as clients complaining about receiving too many e-mails first thing Monday morning) work that feedback into your cadence. Just keep in mind that these are all about keeping the wheel spinning and the momentum going.

E-Mail Automation

Most of us have received an e-mail from someone we do not know addressing us by name and asking us for a meeting. Chances are, they did not write that e-mail and send it just to us. They used one of many e-mail automation systems. This is technology that combines template e-mails and lists of contacts to send what seem to be personal, one-to-one e-mails. It can be incredibly effective for generating engaged, converted, and advocate attention when used right.

The first thing to know is that there is a difference between sales e-mails and marketing e-mails. Sales e-mails, like the one referenced above, have different rules, which we will cover in the next section. Marketing e-mail automation is different because it primarily focuses on people and contacts you already know or interacted with or those who have given you permission to contact them. There are some very powerful and common-sense use cases for e-mail automation:

Customers—Depending on your business, your customers may already hear from your team regularly about the business you are doing together. But they may not hear from the company's leadership directly. You can e-mail them feedback surveys, ask them for a quality check-in call, ask them for feedback on a new product or service, ask them to develop content with you, or ask them for referrals. Your first e-mail in the automated series may introduce yourself or a member of your leadership team if they are not already acquainted. The second e-mail, automatically scheduled to go days or weeks later, may ask them for a favor or give them an offer. The third e-mail may just thank them for their help and assistance and let them know they can contact you at any time with questions or concerns. This methodology of friendly follow-up and reminders can also be used by e-commerce companies who are trying to get people to buy things they have put in their shopping carts. All of these conversations are focused on engagement and can go a long way toward keeping attention over time.

Centers of Influence—There are people who send you business. They care about you and your organization. They want to help. Unfortunately, most companies do not have a plan to keep their attention and stay top-of-mind with them. Automated e-mail marketing can help close that gap. We have had a lot of success using e-mail automation even with a small group of contacts. On a regular basis, we send them e-mails that give them early access to new whitepapers or eBooks, provide them free tickets to events for them and a guest, ask them for catch-up calls, share new insights or research with them, or share case study information with them in case they know companies that have similar challenges to our clients. Rarely do we ask for business or referrals directly. But when we keep information flowing to them in a way that seems personal, we see a return on this relatively easy and automated approach.

Suppliers—Your suppliers have a vested interest in your success. However, most companies never consider them a marketing audience. E-mail automation is a relatively easy way to close this gap. Set up a segmented list of your most important suppliers and send them regular one-to-one e-mails that outline what you are working on, what your plans are, and what your goals are. Invite them to have conversations with you and your team about ways you can partner more effectively and go after business together. Once again, offer to create content together with them and share it with your collective audiences. Your e-mails to them should be inspiring, since you want to make them your advocates.

Long-Term Prospects—The automated check-in with long-term prospects or those who have given you a "not right now" answer is one of the most effective uses of e-mail automation. It should be all about getting them from connected attention back to engaged attention when the time is right. These e-mails can be triggered at different times depending on their behavior and how they interact with your e-mails. They can be a simple and straightforward "is now a good time to re-engage" e-mail to something more complicated asking for their feedback or thoughts. Just be friendly, kind, and human, and you will see returns from this effort over time.

Compliance

E-mail marketing has rules. In fact, these rules come from the federal government, and breaking them can trigger penalties over $40,000. These rules are sometimes updated, so be sure to regularly check on Google for updates. If you are using an e-mail marketing technology, they should also share alerts with you. Here are some general guidelines:

1. **Do not have misleading information in the FROM field or subject line.** Your e-mails should be what they are and not anything else. It is a general rule for good marketing, too.
2. **Identify that the message is marketing.** Do not pretend it is an account update or security alert if it is not.
3. **Let people know where you are.** You must have a real, physical address at the bottom of your e-mails so people can look you up if they want, make sure you are real, and contact you if they think that is necessary.
4. **Let them unsubscribe.** Put a link at the bottom of your e-mail so they can stop getting them if they want to and make sure you respect

their request. Most e-mail marketing technologies require this before they let you send an e-mail, but this is the thing that really gets companies in trouble.

E-mail is a constantly moving target. Lots of systems exist to stop marketing messages from getting delivered. Lots of people are also working to make sure e-mails still get delivered. It is a constant push-and-pull. If you are going to use it as a core part of your surround sound marketing, just be sure you are researching it regularly and staying on top of changes.

Overlaps

The thing about surround sound is that it works best when PR, e-mail, and social media work together to get, keep, and use attention. There are some other tactical things you can do to get more out of them.

Media placements make great social media posts and e-mail content. When your PR team is working well, you will have regular media placements about your company, your thought leaders, your products, services, events, and so on. But media placements are only as good as the people who see them. It is your job to make sure that the right people see them. Post them on all your social media channels. Perhaps even put dollars behind them to promote them in front of your current and desired audiences. Include media placements in your newsletter or even send out a special alert if the placement is significant. Your audiences will appreciate the credibility of the media coverage. It may even excite and inspire them. Media coverage that creates awareness can generate the other four types of attention when used well.

Social media can be used to collect e-mail addresses. The list of ideas shared in the e-mail marketing part of this book includes some ways to generate e-mail addresses from social media, but there are others as well. LinkedIn contacts and connections can be turned into e-mail contacts with permission, for sure. But the best and most effective way to get the e-mail address of your social media followers is contests and giveaways. Even B2B organizations can take advantage of voting and charitable promotions to generate e-mails. This is often very effective because it turns surface-level connected attention into more meaningful, deeply connected attention that feeds the flywheel of surround sound.

E-mail addresses can be used in targeted social media advertising. There is a type of advertising through Facebook, Instagram, LinkedIn, Twitter, and others called "custom audiences" or something similar depending on the platform. If you have one thousand e-mail addresses or more, you can input them into the advertising platform and target social media ads to those same people. This means when they log into their social media accounts, they see your content and information. These ads tend to do very well because there is already awareness and connected attention. Once the ads have been served for a while, the social media platforms learn about this audience and you can target people just like them in what is often called "lookalike audiences." Custom and lookalike audiences often have the best return on investment for social media advertising.

We have no doubt there are other ways you can find within your organization to create surround sound by getting PR, social media, and e-mail marketing to work together. When you do this and do it well, your marketing success will grow exponentially.

PART II

Execution

CHAPTER 7

Getting Alignment

How to Ensure Your Internal Stakeholders Are on the Same Page

Great marketing communications supports the growth of the company. However, many marketers don't take the time to understand what the company really needs in order to be successful in the next 12 to 18 months. Worse, sales, HR, product development, customer service, finance, and others work in silos without involving marketing at all in their planning, their research, and their outreach.

Before tackling this issue, we should make sure we're "aligned" on "alignment." The term itself is thrown around with other boardroom jargon without much thought. But at its core, alignment means agreement: getting all of your teams on the same page, working toward the same goal, understanding the same challenges, opportunities, and strategies. If information isn't flowing freely and plans aren't shared across departments, you could encounter duplicative work, contradictory messaging, and general inefficiencies across the board.

To get ahead of this, consider utilizing the information gathering exercise outlined in this chapter. By getting all of the necessary stakeholders around the table, marketers will understand what each invested party wants—and what the company needs—in order to achieve success. This could be a big ask: Not all stakeholders will inherently understand the value of a session like this. Some may be too busy to block the time, others just won't prioritize marketing. If you find yourself in a situation where you're receiving a lot of pushback, don't be afraid to use scare tactics. By that we mean, clearly explain the risks of not participating.

We once worked with a client that was planning a massive, nationwide announcement about their company's structure, service, and branding. It was an enormous event for their company and their customers alike. Our team was tasked with supporting the internal marketing team, but we were given strict instructions not to engage other departments or vendors. We found ourselves in a bit of an information silo and we relied solely on what the internal marketing team communicated to us. Apparently, the internal marketing team itself was experiencing a similar silo. Without the product, research and finance departments having alignment meetings with marketing, the launch date quickly approached ... and passed. Months of hard work and planning, from detailed timelines to large scale creative campaigns, were rendered obsolete. It turns out that the company was nowhere near ready to make the announcement. On top of that, they had already maxed out their budget. Missed deadlines, unmet goals, and overspending are all very real consequences of misalignment.

So how do you avoid this kind of catastrophe? Start by identifying if your company follows a top-down or bottom-up methodology for setting priorities. Companies with a strong-willed CEO who is very involved in sales and marketing are often top-down. Companies led by servant-leaders who are more involved with finance, operations, or delivery are often bottom-up. Whatever the case, you need to figure out which one yours is.

To determine this, we ask new clients to take a Communication Self-Assessment survey whenever we begin work. This questionnaire consists of 40 pairs of statements based on Pierre Casse's *Training for the Cross-Cultural Mind* (1979, 125–132). The client is to select one statement from each pair that is most typical of his or her personality. No pair is an either-or proposal, meaning the statements are unrelated, and choices should be made as spontaneously as possible. This exercise takes less than five minutes, but it helps us a great deal by categorizing our points of contact as either Action, Process, Idea, or People communicators.

Action communicators tend to focus on results, objectives, and productivity. They're direct and decisive, but quick to jump from idea to idea and often considered impatient. Process communicators center the conversation around facts, procedures, and analysis. They want to see the proof, read the plans, and test, test, test! Because of this, they can be seen as controlling or cautious. Idea communicators believe in innovation, creative concepts, and imagination. Others interpret their behavior as provocative or independent. People communicators are focused on motivation, cooperation, and values. They're empathetic, subjective, and can be more spontaneous than the other types of communicators.

More often than not, Action CEOs are Top-Down, and people CEOs are bottom-up (see Figure 7.1). We've seen process and idea go both ways, but idea tends to skew more top-down and process bottom-up.

Once you determine the methodology, you will need to set up individual alignment meetings with the strategy stakeholders (see Figure 7.2). If your colleagues balk at the term "alignment," call it a "touch base" or "check in," or whatever language they're more comfortable with. Here are two examples and a worksheet you can use to outline your own approach to alignment. For the purposes of this book, we chose the customer and client audience type. If the audiences are different, the stakeholders included will be different.

Try to complete your meetings within two weeks so you have the most up-to-date information all at once. Then, it's time to do the research.

Figure 7.1 Top-down bottom-up model

Sample alignment meeting agenda

The first meeting is with...

Because:

The goal of the meeting is:

I need to ask:

Date / time / location:

The ☐ meeting is with...

Because:

The goal of the meeting is:

I need to ask:

Date / time / location:

Figure 7.2 Sample alignment meeting agenda

How are you doing? How have you done historically? Are there any data sources that you have that show that you've made progress toward these things? If not, what data sources do you need in the future? This research from past performance will ensure that you are keeping what works and leaving behind what doesn't.

What does it look like when it all comes together? Goals are achieved! Records are broken! Growth benchmarks are surpassed! One of our clients in particular is a golden example of successful alignment. The marketing team has a seat at every table in every meeting so that they can connect the dots and offer potential solutions. They're respected within the organization because time and time again, they've been able to break down silos and prioritize the biggest company challenges. When the company needed to attract new talent, the marketing team followed the top-down methodology and conducted information-gathering sessions with the CEO, HR, and the departments that needed to staff up. Everyone bought into their marketing strategy and provided the content required (employee spotlights, company culture highlights, etc.) to hit the ground running. The marketing team provided succinct, consistent updates to all of the stakeholders involved, and within a month of launch, they were reporting increased applications from a diverse, qualified pool of potential employees.

Regardless of the goal, it's safe to assume that there's no time to waste. Having these alignment meetings will keep you focused, resourced, and effective.

CHAPTER 8

Making a Plan

Making Sure Your Marketing Strategies Are Actionable

Few marketing and communications professionals have a strategic planning and execution routine. It's like getting a good night's sleep—we all know we should do it, some have created good habits, and many of us have not. We all know that we should have a tempo, timeline, and a process for doing research, creating a strategy, executing the strategy, checking it regularly, adjusting it occasionally, and reviewing it thoroughly. We know that it will help us become better marketers, get bigger budgets, and show more value to our companies. We also face the reality of doing a million little things that aren't in the strategy while trying to keep up with all the changes in our industry.

In this chapter, we've outlined some actionable steps and shared templates that will help your entire marketing team create a plan and stick to it over the course of the year. Of course, some companies work on a three-year plan while others need to change course every six months. All these exercises, and more importantly the thinking behind them, will still be valuable as you work through the alignment, strategy, execution, measurement, analysis, and adjustment cycle (see Figure 8.1).

Marketing communications is part art and part science. It is notoriously hard to know exactly what is working and what is not. But with a regular approach to setting and achieving goals, all marketers will have the opportunity to learn and grow.

There are many different approaches to developing a marketing communications strategy. Just Google the topic and millions of templates will be right at your fingertips. Whatever approach you use, know that leaders

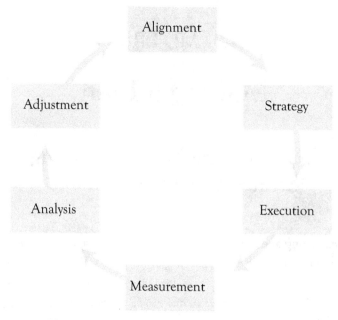

Figure 8.1 Alignment and adjustment cycle

simplify, delegate, predict, systematize, and structure. A good strategy that can be executed will do all those things.

From a content perspective, we have found that the best strategies have these parts:

- **Findings/Research**—What have you learned during the discovery period? Start with the basics here: What is the challenge at hand? Then delve into what's currently working and not working in the form of a company audit. Evaluate your social media channels, e-mail communications, and media coverage. Next, turn to your competitors. Who is doing an exceptional job, and where? Conversely, where are your competitors slipping up and leaving an opportunity for you? All of this research and analysis will be the foundation of your recommendations.
- **Description of Priority Audiences**—Who is it that you're trying to reach? Another way to phrase this: Who must you communicate with in order to be successful? Revisit *Chapter*

2: The Six Audiences Who Matter; The People Whose Attention You Need for clarity if needed, as this is one of the most important sections to nail down before continuing.

- **What Success Looks Like (alignment around types of attention)**—Maybe your audience is aware of your company but they haven't connected in a meaningful way. Perhaps they are engaging with you online but not taking that next step to convert. Decide where you need to focus, realizing that you have to move from left to right through the model. We can't tackle conversion if no one is aware of your brand. Make sure all stakeholders are aligned on this and understand the focus.

- **Measurable Marketing Communications Goals**—Track your different types of attention back to measurable actions. If you're focused on building awareness, your key performance indicators should be around impressions, reach, and viewership of coverage. If you're aiming for advocate attention, you can measure testimonials created, shares of your content in industry groups, or influencers engaged. Again, make sure stakeholders are aligned on how you're tracking progress here, and that they understand you're reporting on marketing efforts' impact.

- **Messages and Content**—Based on all of the aforementioned, what are the core messages you need to convey to your targeted audience? How will you position your company to them in a way that resonates? What values do you share with your target audience? Capture this as succinctly as possible, and then imagine how these "north stars" will drive content creation.

- **Tactics to Achieve the Goals (public relations, social media, e-mail marketing, events, advertising, SEO, etc.)**— Get into the nitty gritty, channel by channel breakdown here. How many times should you be posting on social media per week? Which hashtags should you be using? Build your media lists, outline your news hooks, and research thought leadership opportunities like industry awards. Decide on the cadence of broadcast e-mails and design the triggers for automated e-mails. This section should be considered the playbook, so any member of the marketing team could pick it up and understand how to execute the plan.

- **Creative Campaigns (try something new)**—Break the mold and think big. How can you bring your positioning statement and point of view to life? If you find yourself saying, "we tried that in the past and…" stop right there. Bring in other departments for fresh perspectives and fun brainstorms. Think back to your competitive analysis and see if you can build off of any creative ideas that you discovered from research.

- **Standard Operating Procedures**—How will the work get done? For all of the process communicators, this section is incredibly important. Identify how often you'll meet, with whom, and how reporting is to be delivered. Outline in black and white so that, once again, everyone is aligned in terms of expectations.

- **Assignment of Roles and Accountabilities**—Make sure all stakeholders understand their role, even if it is just to approve content before posting. Have a clear outline of who is responsible for which deliverables, and when.

- **Gut Check (will everything we're proposing actually help us get the attention we need?)**—As self-explanatory as this sounds, it's good to build this into your template. It's a forced pause to say, "Do we agree this is worth testing?" before moving forward.

The simpler the strategy is, the better it will be understood by everyone involved. All the people that were interviewed in the alignment process should be presented the strategy and given an opportunity to provide additional insight. Those involved in execution should be as well. But as the marketing leader, you should have the final say. This strategy outline will continue to be a powerful tool long after it's presented. It's a document that all stakeholders can reference at any time, but it's also a tool for you to take back to the table if expectations get cloudy down the line.

We once worked with a client that was sold on strategy and enthusiastic to begin work. About three months into our engagement, he shared that he was disappointed that we weren't seeing more conversions. Rather than have a long, awkward conversation, we were able to bring up the strategy deck and reference the "What Success Looks Like" and "Measurable Marketing Goals" section. It was an easy reminder that we had to establish awareness before we could work our way down to converted attention. And when we revisited our awareness goals, we were able to show real growth in those key metrics over the course of three months.

It's also helpful to revisit the Creative Campaigns from time to time. We've had plenty of clients where at first, the campaigns seemed out of reach, but six months in, budgets had changed and timing felt right. It's another reason to reference this core document early and often.

Execution can take different forms depending on the business goals and the marketing strategy. There are three things that get in the way of successful execution:

1. **Lack of Clarity About Accountability**—Conflicts occur when people don't know their lanes or refuse to stay in them. We recommend that an Accountability Chart is created in the Roles and Accountabilities section of every strategy. If there are conflicts, this should help resolve them quickly.
2. **Lack of Capacity**—Too often, marketing people bite off more than they can chew. Do not be afraid to ask for more resources or reconsider priorities as execution is underway. We've also created an easy-to-use Agency Selection Organizer you can find at the end of this chapter if you need to add some outside help.
3. **Distractions**—Marketing people are often expected to do everything from writing proposals to planning baby showers to hosting team building events. Yes, we're great at a lot of things. But that can prevent us from doing what brings our companies the most value. Do not be afraid to say no. Or hire more staff to help!

So, what does it take to follow the marketing communications strategy cycle well? It looks something like this (see Figure 8.2).

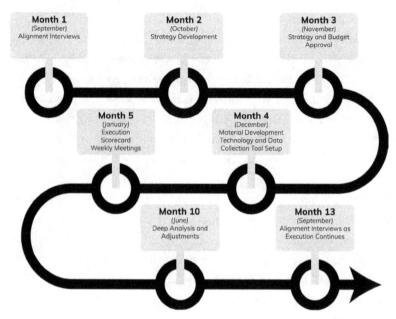

Figure 8.2 Marketing strategy calendar

When You Cannot Do It All

There are times when you do not have the skills, capacity, or budget to get the job done internally. But how do you know whether an agency is right for you? This Agency Selection Organizer (see Figure 8.3) will help you ask and answer the questions that are the most critical for selecting an agency that will help you achieve your marketing goals.

Agency selection organizer

Company overview

```
┌─────────────────────────────────────────────────────┐
│                                                       │
│                                                       │
│                                                       │
│                                                       │
└─────────────────────────────────────────────────────┘
```

Target audiences
Our primary target audience is:

```
┌─────────────────────────────────────────────────────┐
│                                                       │
│                                                       │
│                                                       │
│                                                       │
└─────────────────────────────────────────────────────┘
```

Other relevant audiences include:

```
┌─────────────────────────────────────────────────────┐
│                                                       │
│                                                       │
│                                                       │
│                                                       │
└─────────────────────────────────────────────────────┘
```

Trade associations and groups include:

```
┌─────────────────────────────────────────────────────┐
│                                                       │
│                                                       │
│                                                       │
│                                                       │
└─────────────────────────────────────────────────────┘
```

Competitors in our market include:

```
┌─────────────────────────────────────────────────────┐
│                                                       │
│                                                       │
│                                                       │
│                                                       │
└─────────────────────────────────────────────────────┘
```

Brand guidelines and marketing infrastructure

Website / CRM

```
┌───────────────────────┐
│                       │
│                       │
│                       │
└───────────────────────┘
```

Website analytics

```
┌───────────────────────┐
│                       │
│                       │
│                       │
└───────────────────────┘
```

Social media channels

```
┌───────────────────────┐
│                       │
│                       │
│                       │
└───────────────────────┘
```

Email marketing tool

```
┌───────────────────────┐
│                       │
│                       │
│                       │
└───────────────────────┘
```

Brand guidelines

```
┌───────────────────────┐
│                       │
│                       │
│                       │
└───────────────────────┘
```

Other tools

```
┌───────────────────────┐
│                       │
│                       │
│                       │
└───────────────────────┘
```

Agency selection organizer

Services required
We are seeking an agency partner that can provide...

[   ]

Goals
We are looking for an agency partner to help us generate this type of attention:

□ Awareness   □ Converted attention
□ Connected attention   □ Advocacy
□ Engaged attention

Our company has some immediate marketing priorities that include...

[   ]

Our total, inclusive budget for the marketing services listed, as well as out-of-pocket expenses, production costs, etc. is

[   ]

The budget is intended to cover the following timeframe:

[   ]

We will be evaluating an agency partner based on these criteria:

[   ]

Figure 8.3 Agency Selection Organizer

CHAPTER 9

Measuring Success

Marketing Will Always Be About Learning and Changing

Measurement

Too often, marketing goals sit in a strategy never to be reviewed again. That's a disaster. Worse still, there are no defined marketing goals.

We work with lots of companies and executives who have no idea what success looks like for them. We ask them, "If we're sitting here a year from now high-fiving because the marketing effort has been so successful—what does that look like?" There are only three real answers. The most common is that people have no idea. They have never been asked the question or even really thought about the answer. The second most likely answer is some sort of vague, unrealistic definition of success that is along the lines of, "We are on the *Today Show*," or "Gary Vee tweets about us," or "Our brand is more well-respected." None of these are good goals. The least common answer is, "We will increase our brand awareness metrics by 20 percent with a focus on our most profitable client type," or something along those lines.

All marketing departments should have SMART goals at the beginning of each year: specific, measurable, attainable, relevant, and time-bound. Everyone should agree on them (see *Chapter 7: Getting Alignment*) and know how they benefit the overall business goals. They should be based on data and supported by budget allocations. Most importantly, they should be reviewed regularly. Everyone in the marketing organization should know if they are being achieved or not and should be able to answer for them if asked any day of the week.

That is why we recommend a weekly scorecard (see Figure 9.1). The scorecard will keep the team focused on the most important things that the entire company has decided are critical. All the metrics should be weekly metrics. Let us say that one of your results goals is 10 inbound leads per month. Your weekly metric would be 2.5. If your quarterly goal is to post four new blogs, the weekly goal is 0.3. Go through every goal and set a metric that everyone agrees is both reasonable and somewhat aspirational.

Sample scorecards

Objective: Awareness goal	Accountability	Timeframe	Week 1
Impression on social channels	Social media		
UVPM from media mentions	Public relations		
Emails delivered	Email marketing		

Objective: Connected Attention goal	Accountability	Timeframe	Week 1
Impression on social channels	Social media		
Pitches to the media	Public relations		
Emails subscribers	Email marketing		

Objective: Engaged Attention goal	Accountability	Timeframe	Week 1
Engagements on social channels	Social media		
Conversation with reporters	Public relations		
Emails opens	Email marketing		

Objective: Converted Attention goal	Accountability	Timeframe	Week 1
Clicks from social channels	Social media		
Media placements	Public relations		
Emails delivered	Email marketing		

Objective: Advocacy goal	Accountability	Timeframe	Week 1
Uses of hashtags / post tags	Social media		
Media mentions outside of pitching	Public relations		
Emails forwards	Email marketing		

Figure 9.1 Five sample scorecards for each type of attention

This is where it is critical to have marketing measurement infrastructure in place. If you already have it, look at the past six months to identify the benchmark. Then add a certain percentage to the baseline to create the metric. The metric can be for the year (in which case you divide it by 52), half a year (divide by 26), a quarter (13), or a month (4). If you don't have data for a metric, use an educated guess. Then ensure you can measure it moving forward. If you cannot measure something, it is not a good goal.

Once you have the goals and the metrics, the last part is accountability. Each goal should be assigned to a person who will take accountability for achieving and reporting it. No, this does not mean that the person needs to do all the work themselves. But they are responsible for the outcome, either positive or negative.

Ideally, you will do most of this work during the strategy development process. But you should look at the scorecard weekly in order to know what is working and what is not.

Analysis

What makes one tactic, message, or campaign successful and another one an abject failure? It's hard to know. It could be the time of year, the wrong audience, or not enough investment. True analysis requires a tremendous amount of humility and self-awareness. Many businesspeople—not just marketers—have a lot of trouble with this.

We once worked with a global corporation that asked us to review their social media efforts and give them feedback on what was working well and what was not. They had data, delivered reports monthly, and could even show trends over time. We began by asking them about their audiences. Social media, you see, is about people. So, we wanted to know what people mattered to them. We needed to understand what those people wanted from them and what they wanted from those people. That was the only way we could analyze the data. No analysis can exist without intention and context.

After a while, we started to understand what they wanted to achieve with their social media effort, and we helped them move beyond just doing social media to do it. We got them thinking about the types of attention they needed and from whom they needed that attention. Then, we could see from the data whether or not they were getting it. We could understand what resonated with them, what the audience engaged with or was interested in. It was easy to identify what either did not work at all or what worked for people who followed them but were not their priorities. From there, they could start to do better.

Pretty soon after doing this analysis regularly, they started to change their focus and got the results they wanted. The people they cared about started paying attention. Those connected started to engage. Advocates became easier to identify. And their C-Suite noticed. They were recognized for their work helping the company more effectively communicate, listen, and show they cared.

The lesson here is that analysis is not about blame. It's about learning. And if you ask Brené Brown, most learning comes from having the courage to be vulnerable. Analysis is about vulnerability. As marketing people, what we do and how we do it changes every day. Thanks, Facebook. And Twitter. And Google Analytics. And WordPress. And Microsoft. And Alexa. And how people generally interact with technology. And ….

Since deep analysis takes a lot of courage, it cannot be done well every day. Or every month. Or every quarter. We need some distance. For that reason, we recommend a true review every six months or at the completion of a creative campaign. Any more than that, and we will likely make ourselves and everyone else around us crazy.

Adjustment

Little adjustments can happen weekly in response to the scorecard. We should always be working to do better, get more media coverage, make our ads more compelling, make our blogs more interesting. Big adjustments should occur no more than every six months following a thorough analysis and conversations with leadership.

Of course, we also need to be reactive to big changes in the company. A merger, bankruptcy of a major competitor, shift in the economy, production problems, personnel changes, and so on can all necessitate a major change in our strategy. We need to be flexible enough to adjust to those things.

At the same time, we cannot be reactive. We've found that the best approach is to go into maintenance mode—focus on the basics of engaging your most important targeted audiences—while sorting out the new strategy and approach. **Never, ever go dark**, even if it means outsourcing everything while putting all your effort into what's next for the company.

CHAPTER 10

Building a Marketing Team

A Strategy Is Only as Good as the People Who Execute It

There are a million different ways to structure a marketing department. That is because marketing can mean so many different things to so many different people and companies. The reality is that most marketing is planned and executed ineffectually. This is a big problem because a marketing department with the wrong structure can significantly prohibit a company's growth.

The opportunity cost is enormous. How can people buy from you if they don't know your company exists? How can they buy from you when they're not clear on what you sell, or how it adds value to their lives? How can they buy from you if your products or services are forgettable? Or worse, if your brand is? How can they buy from you if your website doesn't let them contact you easily? Or if they're away from their desks the moments you reply and you never contact them again? Why would someone buy from you if you're exactly the same as a competitor?

Yes, there is a lot to marketing. No, you can't do it all. But with the right team focused on the most important priorities at every phase of your company's growth and development, a marketing department can deliver tremendous results and be a major driver of success.

There is no definitive structure for a marketing department. There are no must-have positions that work for every company. There is no handbook. Every department in every company is different because there will never be one standardized set of targeted audiences. There will never be one way to buy. These are the realities of marketing. It's also the fun. Things are always changing. Marketers can always try something new. And every day is different from the last.

The Symptoms

There are a number of underlying behaviors, activities, and blind spots that may be an indication that a marketing department is not set up to be successful. Before you read the rest of this book, you must be honest about whether your company has one or more of these issues. If you skip this step, you are destined to repeat the same mistakes over and over with different people in different roles. These fundamental issues will always affect the effectiveness of a marketing team.

- "Marketing" really means sales support. If all the marketing department does is put together proposals and presentations for the sales team, it's not actually marketing. There's nothing wrong with sales support professionals. Some of our favorite people are in sales support. But they're not marketing people. Let's not pretend.

- The department is a dumping ground for family members. Sure, we may all have had a cousin who interned for an agency one summer. Cass can admit it. Her cousin is great and even works in marketing now. But, despite popular opinion, not everyone can "do marketing." It's not just designing a logo and throwing parties. In fact, it's rarely either of those things. So just because the boss's daughter planned her own wedding or knows how to use Twitter doesn't mean she should be a member of a professional marketing team. You deserve better.

- Your weekly to-dos include ordering lunch and planning baby showers. Somehow, people who work in the finance or information technology department never get asked to run out and get lunch for the client who showed up without notice. No one asks the janitorial team to make cupcakes or pick out favors for a baby shower. These unnoticed, unrewarded, nonstrategic burdens almost always fall on marketing, administrative, or HR professionals. Yes, we are good at these things. No, we can't do them; we actually perform a critical role in the company that is just as important as any other.

- No one has any real education or experience in marketing. This is similar to the second symptom. No, marketing is not easy. No, not everyone can do it. Cass worked with an organization for years that put people who otherwise would have been on disability leave in the marketing department. They spent lots of money on outside agencies just to get anything done.

- There are no annual measurable marketing goals. As the old saying goes, you can't manage what you can't measure. If there are no clearly defined marketing goals, there is a fundamental problem. It could be the way the company operates: Perhaps nothing is measured at the company. It could be a lack of accountability from marketing leadership. If it is the latter, there must be a change in leadership prior to making any other changes to the department.

- Marketing doesn't have a seat at the table. This is by far the most problematic offense. In order to be effective, a marketing team representative must be involved in all of the company's leadership decisions. Fast-growing companies know their market. They refine their messages. They understand their competitors. They make decisions about marketing and spend based on data and analytics. Marketing, when functioning well, brings all these things to the company's table. If these conversations aren't with the marketing team's involvement, the department will never add real value to the organization.

Lastly, if a CEO doesn't value marketing, it will never work. No amount of time, energy, or money will solve this issue. (Cass has written an eBook on this topic that you can access on the Slice Communications website for your CEO if they fall into that category.) The company will hopefully find other ways to grow, but it should not invest in marketing when leadership doesn't believe in it.

The following exercise can be used to identify where your strengths are related to your priorities (see Figure 10.1).

Marketing department effectiveness

The area where we are adding the most value to the business is:

```


```

The area where we could easily add additional value to the business is:

```


```

The area where we would need to make a lot of changes in order to add value to the business is:

```


```

The area where we need to do the most capacity building is:

```


```

Evaluating the Current Team

This is perhaps the trickiest part. It's also the most important. Most marketing people are super nice. They're great to be around. They're good for culture. And no one wants to fire them.

Marketing department effectiveness

Priority business goal #1:

Activities	Goal results and metrics	Resources dedicated today	Effectiveness today (1–10)

Priority business goal #2:

Activities	Goal results and metrics	Resources dedicated today	Effectiveness today (1–10)

Figure 10.1 Marketing department effectiveness worksheet

Many are also completely ineffective. It's not always their fault. A lack of strategy, under-resourcing, distractions, and bad direction can all account for a marketing employee who is not living up to their full potential. The bad news is that there's no place in a well-run marketing department for someone who does not add value or brings the wrong skillset. That's particularly true in fast-growing businesses.

There are two worksheets we've developed to determine whether someone can contribute appropriately to the future of the company and the department.

The first is the Marketing Team Member Skills and Experience worksheet (see Figure 10.2). There are two insights to be gained from this

Marketing team skills and expertise

Part 1 - your skills, expertise, and interests

My marketing skills	Value these add to the business	Percentage of my time at work now	Additional resources needed

Part 2 - The company's priorities

Which of the following should be the company's priorities in the next 12–18 months (select 2)?
- ☐ Awareness
- ☐ Connected attention
- ☐ Engaged attention
- ☐ Converted attention
- ☐ Advocacy

Which of the marketing communications activities on the following page are the most important in order for the company to achieve the business goals? (select no more than five)

If you could wave a magic wand and make our marketing department 20 times more effective, what would you do?

Figure 10.2 Marketing team member skills and expertise worksheet

exercise. First, it becomes glaringly obvious whether the team member filling it out "gets it" and is aligned with what the company needs. Second, it will help you and that person figure out if their skills are necessary in a full-time role in the company. The worksheet should be sent electronically to the team member for completion. Do not send the business goals (see Figure 10.3) you've identified or any of the other work you've done. It is important that this is done only with the experience and insight the person has gained to date.

Needed skills and expertise

Use as many of the following boxes as necessary to group the listed activities by function:

Finally, give each box a name or title that best describes the functional group.

Needed skills and expertise

1. In order to achieve our business goals, our marketing department today needs to ... (*list all activities*)

2. 12–18 months from now, we will also need to ... (*list all activities*)

Figure 10.3 Needed skills and expertise worksheet

Of course, there is an exception to this rule. If a member of the team has joined in the past 90 days, share the background work and insights you've collected before they do the exercise so that it is fair to them.

Creating a Structure for Scale

Now you know the business goals and activities required to add value, skills of current team members, and functional roles needed for the future. Having established that, it's time to pull it all together in a structure that will scale as your business grows. Take the boxes from the last worksheet and go through these steps:

1. What resources do you need to dedicate in order to make each functional group work? Do you think they will take 10 hours a week? Do you need to invest $500 per month in software?
2. Is there someone on the current team who has the knowledge, capacity, and desire to deliver on every activity in the functional area? If not, is it a priority for the next 12 months? If so, do you think you can find a person to do these activities? Can you outsource this functional area?
3. Can your budget support all the required people, technology, and consultant resources you need? If not, what can be put off until the future?
4. Which functions support the others? Is there a natural reporting structure that makes sense and will be effective?
5. At the end of this work, you should end up with something that looks like Figure 10.4.

From there, you can work with them on readiness. What do their individual LinkedIn profiles look like? What do they say? Have they given any speeches or sat on any panels? Do they see any of those opportunities for themselves? Do they write blogs, articles, anything else? Do they want to? Have they ever given an interview to a reporter? How did it go? Do they like to make videos? Do they know how? Are they comfortable or do they hate the sound of their voices?

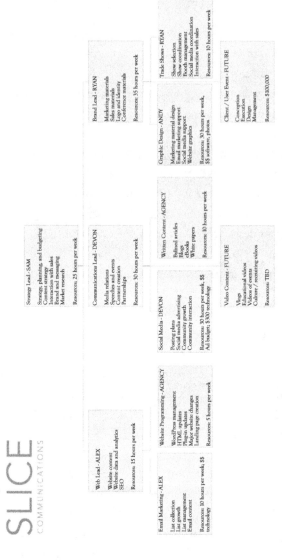

Figure 10.4 Structure for scale

From here, you can craft individual or group training workshops for them on these subjects, as necessary. You should bring in outside consultants and instructors if necessary. Any time and energy you put into your champions will come back tenfold.

In the beginning of this effort, it will likely make sense to bring in outside consultants or facilitators. They should be able to work with marketing, HR, and champions to oversee the execution of the employer brand. Initially, they should be accountable for the goals and objectives until they can be understood and consumed by an internal team member. They should remove barriers and resolve conflicts. Most of all, they should provide focus and guidance. This will go a long way in making sure the employer brand is communicated well.

CHAPTER 11

When You Don't Want Attention

If this chapter seems familiar to you, it is because you may have already read a variation of it in Chapter 7 of Social Media is About a People *also written by us. This is not déjà vu! We know that this information is so central to crisis communications we could not have you miss it, which is why we are including it in this book.*

There are times in your business where you are not going to want attention. This is usually because there is some sort of crisis that has occurred. So, to end the book, let's talk about those times when you do not want attention.

Crises fall into a number of different categories. The first are internal crises, which are things that you can potentially foresee and that you can have a little more control over. You can often have the upper hand in dealing with these crises because you know about them first and you have the most information as it relates to them. Let's say you have a product recall, something has gone wrong with one of your services, you screwed up something for a client or a customer, you are facing financial troubles or a potential bankruptcy, or maybe there is something in one of your policies that has been discriminatory or identified as discriminatory. All of these are scenarios which were caused by you, and are crises that you have the ability to fix internally.

Another type of crisis is one that is caused by people unrelated to you or caused by people who are related to you, but that you do not control. Some of these crises may include some sort of sexual assault or harassment that has happened in your workplace, not by your leadership or by others, but by a vendor you have allowed into your workplace and who provided you with something that is less than up to standard. The crises could even be something where you are associated with an investor group, donor group, or foundation that has gotten into some trouble. These are areas where you cannot control everything; most certainly, you cannot control the message as it relates to all of those things. You also do not have the ability to solely determine the outcome.

The third category of crises are things that are entirely external. Some examples might be if there is a *force majeure* event that interrupts your business or customers. If there is some sort of insurrection, external pandemic, or major financial crisis at a global level, all of these are things that you will likely be forced to deal with, but you do not have any control over. In fact, other than how your company responds, when you are thinking about the types of responses, you need to realize that there are three different audiences to whom you must respond. The first audience, and the one that is the most important, is going to be your internal audience—your employees. In each and every one of these situations, you have to communicate with them and well. Unfortunately, a lot of the time people overlook that because they do not think about their employees as one of their audiences for communications during a crisis. This is a major mistake as your employees are the single most important audience and should be prioritized at all times!

There is never a time when you do not want to talk to your employees through a crisis and you must always make sure that you are communicating with them. Part of the reason you want to do that is because employees are uncertain in a crisis situation and it makes it almost impossible for them to successfully complete their work or be productive if they are not sure what is going to happen. Particularly when they do not obtain clarity and leadership from you about what is going on, or reassurances from you that you are doing everything that you can to handle the crisis, employees will begin to doubt your leadership and effectiveness. Even in those cases where you are communicating well with employees, you are still going to lose some productivity until the crisis resolves. Finally, when you are not communicating with your employees through a crisis, you actually create a communication gap where your employees begin to look to each other for solutions or information. They may even begin to look outside of your company. When you do that, you actually give up even more control in a crisis situation, and that can be detrimental, because the last thing you want to do is give up even more control when you have so little and you are already operating in crisis mode. It's important to make sure that you reinforce your values during a crisis, that you are communicating with your employees regularly, that you are giving them chances to ask you questions, and that you are also giving your management and leadership team information to be able to communicate with their direct reports on a more regular basis. A lot of times, people will trust what they receive from their direct supervisor or boss more than what they hear from the CEO because they work with that direct person—they have a personal relationship with the direct manager and they know them way better than they know the CEO. So when we think about employee communication, it really should be on a parallel path. One is communication regularly with all of the employees and the other part of the parallel path is communication with supervisors and managers who can then share out to the rest of the employees.

The second audience to consider when you are completing your communication plan and must communicate for crises are your ancillary partners. These are people who are involved in, and invested in, the future success of your business. These partners can range from your suppliers, banking partners, lawyer, accountant, members of your accountant's firm, and others you need to continue to believe in you. These partners are looking to you for information and answers and they want to know what is going on because you need to work hand in hand with them to continue to deliver. One of the biggest mistakes we see is that companies never have a list of those contacts. As a matter of fact, they don't even know who those critical partners and suppliers are. Therefore, when it comes time for communication, they are not able to execute crisis communications with partners or at the very least, well. As a result, those partners are often left in the lurch and unsure of the problems that are occurring, and that hurts trust. The lack of communication with partners also creates a vacuum of information where perhaps they are talking to the employees within your company to try to figure out what is happening and those employees are not always equipped to be able to provide those answers to the ancillary partners. It's worth noting that having your ancillary partners look externally for answers during your business crisis leads them to also obtain answers from the media, which is incredibly problematic because that's how misinformation will spread.

The third audience that you definitely need to consider is your external audience. Your external audience is everyone outside of the company—the general public. It is not always necessary to communicate with those people through a crisis. As a matter of fact, there are times when it is better to just be silent. On the other hand, there are times when it is best to communicate and there are times when you can communicate directly while attempting to communicate indirectly.

We get asked a lot about how companies should respond when there is civil unrest such as riots and protests. We also get asked quite a bit about how to respond to major social issues and social movements happening outside the company. These are issues where it is not always important for someone to say something because it could be a circumstance where your company's voice is not additive, supportive, does not make a difference, or does not make a change. In those situations, you may want to be quiet and not say anything at all. Quiet means not only do you not say anything about the issue at hand, but also that any prescheduled posts or typical campaigns be paused or taken down. The reason here being what you do not want to do is sound tone deaf because your actions show that you are continuing to go about your daily lives, without recognizing that there is a major issue happening in your community or in the world.

If you choose to go silent, go completely silent. Do not just not say *anything* about the situation. Do not say anything about anything at all externally. Sometimes, that's an okay reaction. There are times, though, where companies do need to communicate externally, and what we recommend is that the specific communication cannot just happen once. You cannot say one thing once if you are going to address the situation directly, and then pretend like everything is going to be fine from there. Communication in this situation requires regular ongoing communication, messaging about possible initiatives, and a show of if you really are going to stand up and support something. For instance, if your company truly cares about issues related to Black Lives Matter or sexual harassment and discrimination, your statements and actions must show that you intend to meet the needs of those movements.

To prevent misinformation or fake news, if you care about things related to the environment or environmental crisis, school violence, or gun control, and those issues are critical for your business, then when situations happen in the world that negatively impact these areas you should address them directly. Conversely, if your company does not really have a dedicated and focused effort to solving those issues and you just put out a very simple statement that says we stand with you or our thoughts and prayers are with you, without some sort of follow-up initiative, program, donation, or putting your money where your mouth is, then you are going to have a real issue. People will identify that those words are, in some cases, valueless and meaningless to you as they do not have any money or genuine effort or resources behind them. People will also see that your statements are also not necessarily connected to the company's values and are just something that the company thinks that it needs to say in order to say something, because they feel an external pressure that actually does not exist, especially for small and medium-sized businesses. Think really hard as you are considering what to do and say and when to say something as sometimes, it's better to say nothing and make space for voices that actually do need to be heard.

If you are in a situation where there is some sort of external crisis occurring and you decide that you do want to make a comment on it without saying "we stand with you" or "our thoughts and prayers are with you," there are a couple different ways to communicate. For instance, if you want to make an indirect statement related to racial discrimination or discrimination against Lesbian, Gay, Bisexual, Transgender and Queer+ (LGBTQ+) people, you may have some content that you have used previously related to pro-diversity, inclusion, and LGBTQ+ communities. Sometimes the communication is just a picture. Other times, it is just a video. Still more, it could be a full initiative, just not on the day or those days immediately following an extreme crisis. After sometime in the near future, you may want to put out your message to reinforce your values and program and promote it so that people understand who you are and what you stand for in a positive way, not just your reaction to a negative situation. As you are thinking about completing the planning for this, you might want to have a meeting with your leadership team where you sit down and you write out all of the potential crises that you all could experience and then determine a response for those crises if they occur. Will you communicate internally? Will you communicate to your partner? Will you communicate externally, and if you communicate externally, will it be directly or indirectly? Doing some of that planning will put you in a place where when and/or if a crisis does arrive, you are not at a complete loss.

Now, we want to go back and talk a little bit about crises that are of your own creation, whether intentionally or unintentionally. Even though most of the crises may be unintentional, they are still of your own creation. When those come about, there are two primary golden rules of crisis response. The first one is when a crisis happens, you want to validate people's concerns and show action. Absolutely validate concerns! If something has gone terribly wrong, you cannot just say that it has gone wrong, that it does not make sense, everything is fine, or it all worked out. All of those statements will work against you because people know it is not true. Also, when you try to minimize a crisis, you start to bear the responsibility of covering it up and as we know, the cover up is often worse than the crisis itself. Do not put yourself in a position of pretending like a crisis does not exist, trying to cover it up, or even saying things that may be *perceived* as you trying to cover it up because all of that will hurt you.

The second rule is to show action. Showing action means actually doing something about the crisis, such as making a plan to correct the situation, apologizing to people who have been hurt, making up for errors, and actually doing something to compensate those who have been hurt. It is important to also recognize that making things right to the people you may have hurt includes your employees, customers, or overall business. It is critical to remember that recognizing the situation, apologizing for the situation, and making it right is how you will most likely get yourself out of a crisis situation well. Now, with that being said, once again, you cannot communicate one time with a confession of "we are bad, we did it, and here is what we are going to do to make it right." The companies that come out of crises most successfully are the ones that communicate again and again and again and again about what they are actively doing to make the problem right and the reason that particular crisis or problem will never surface again.

If you get in a fight with a pig, you both get muddy, but the pig is happy. In other words, when you are engaging with people or people are trying to engage with you because they think that you're terrible, or what you have done is wrong, you must not engage in that conversation.

That conversation is meant to make you look even worse and it will. What we recommend is that when you are communicating externally and there are people who are trying to bait you into those conversations, you initially respond to them and say we appreciate your concern and that we would like to talk with you directly about the concern. That acknowledges their concern is legitimate and creates an opportunity for an open dialogue. Once you have that open dialogue—a one-on-one together as human beings with a focus on building relationships and finding a solution—then in a lot of cases, you can turn those things around. Now, as the great Taylor Swift once said in her song *Shake It Off*, "haters gonna hate" (Swift 2014). A truer statement has never been spoken, because there are some people who will just never be happy until everybody is covered in mud. For those people, sometimes you just have to acknowledge, especially online with people not having to be who they are and, in some cases, being anonymous, that there are people who are going to be angry and upset and that you will not be able to change their minds. In those situations, you just need to acknowledge that and say, "We cannot make everybody happy nor are we going to strive to make everybody happy." As long as your targeted audiences know that they are your highest priority, you will be okay. The focus and prioritization of audiences will also help you stay focused on what matters through a crisis situation and will help you avoid getting in that fight with a pig.

Our team once worked with a company where the CEO had the same name as a man who was captured on Instagram screaming racist and homophobic slurs at his neighbor. Unfortunately, people thought that this man was our client even though our client had a slightly different name. Our client's son, who was much younger, had the same name as the racist, homophobic person on Instagram. Our client began getting a lot of messages through their website and on the phone, including death threats and other hostile comments. Our client was so concerned that at that point his reputation was really going to be hurt. Our approach was to be very open and authentic in our use of terms and prove beyond any doubt that it was not our client who said those terrible things. We did that by recording a video showing our client and putting it on the client's Facebook and Instagram pages. We also communicated to people the specific values of our client's company, which was vitally important as this was a company that was really focused on family and continues to be. We helped them draft a diversity statement that they could use for the rest of their existence. That statement was true to their core company values and their actions repeatedly reinforced that. We put up that statement as the primary pop up or primary window when you hit their homepage and we communicated it regularly. Over the course of a couple of days, we significantly decreased the amount of negative volume that was coming to ruin their reputation. So summarily, by communicating with video authentically, honestly, and humanely and then also reinforcing the company's values through diversity inclusion statements, we helped the client take back their reputation quickly.

Another situation with clients that did not go the way it should have was related to the Executive Director of a nonprofit who was accused of sexual harassment and misconduct. Initially, the Executive Director denied the allegations. This individual kept a lot of things secret, but these allegations continued coming out. There were more and more and more accusations and the situation began snowballing out of control. The mistakes that he made at that time were not being completely open and honest about what was going on, which led to us not knowing the whole story. We like to say that there are three people from whom you keep no secrets: your lawyer, your Priest/Rabbi/Spiritual Leader, and your PR people. Tell your PR people everything, because if they don't know everything, they can't create a communication plan for everything. Leaving out information places your PR people in a position where they can't do their best work to help you. The last thing you want to do is surprise your PR people because they can't make sure that they are thinking ahead for you, communicating ahead for you, or being proactive for you.

CHAPTER 12

Becoming an Attention Marketer

We've been working in marketing communications for over 20 years combined, and the thing we love most about our jobs is that we get to ask questions for a living. We firmly believe that asking the right questions is the secret to great marketing because it leads to understanding.

This book has a lot of answers. It has "four of this" and "five of those"—all the systems, processes, and frameworks you could use to build a strong, focused marketing communications strategy. It even has tips, tools, and worksheets to execute the strategy well while engaging thought leaders and employees. All of these things are deceiving, though, because they are not specific or contextual for you or your organization. You should not let all these answers get in the way of the questions you need to ask and answer before you start doing anything.

We have always said that the best marketers are those who are good at saying something compelling. They have a knack for getting people to take action. But this power is useless without understanding. Great marketers will ask about the actions the business needs people to take. They ask a lot of questions about the people the business needs to take these actions. They ask the organizational leaders and then the people themselves even more questions. They never stop asking questions. In every meeting with every person, they ask more and more. They seek deeper and deeper understanding. They also understand that situations and people change all the time. It is their desire to know about those changes before they occur. They yearn to understand the impact of internal and external forces and how they need to make constant adjustments.

Asking the right questions of the right people at the right time requires significant emotional intelligence (EQ). EQ is often defined as "the capacity to be aware of, control, and express one's emotions, and to handle interpersonal relationships judiciously and empathetically" (National Customer Service Association n.d.).

Imagine you are sitting with someone, asking them questions about their division's business goals for the coming year. As you do, you see their shoulders rise up, their face drop, their eyes look away, and their fists tighten. You notice it, but you keep asking and you get short, direct answers without any excitement or enthusiasm. You leave the meeting, work on a marketing plan for the coming year focused on the type of attention they say they need. When you present it, all you get is skepticism, reasons it will not work, and general pushback. You try to execute the plan, but your team never gets what you need from the business unit leader and it fails. Every meeting throughout the year is tense and there is no progress made. All of those working on the marketing effort are demoralized, and some quit. Marketing loses credibility.

Return to that first meeting. What if—instead of asking your prepared questions, you stopped when you saw the leader's body language change? Instead of continuing to ask your marketing questions, you asked if the leader was okay. You let them talk. You heard what was actually going on. You found out there was no way that they could meet the demand of the previous year let alone have the suppliers to meet increased demand. What they really needed was more people, but they kept losing potential employees to the competitor. You would create a very different marketing communications plan with a different priority audience intended to get a different type of attention.

Communication is hard. Doing it poorly starts wars, ends marriages, and costs billions of dollars. Right or wrong, marketers and leaders with strong marketing skills bear the responsibility of ensuring that they are communicating well inside and outside of the company. It is expected that we identify breakdowns in communication and provide solutions even when we are neither responsible nor directly involved. It will never be listed in our job descriptions, and yet it is one of the most important things we contribute to our organizations. We are expected to do it well even when we are stressed, busy, and under tremendous pressure.

Good communication comes from EQ. So does good questioning, not to mention real understanding. Handling relationships—internally and externally—means we need to be aware of how we "show up" in every situation every day.

The big secret of this book is that it will be used well by those with strong EQ and misused by those with little. So before you do anything, take a minute. Are you prepared to control your emotions as you introduce the "Pay Attention!" concepts to your colleagues and team? Even if they do not understand them at first? Even if they get rejected or are misunderstood at first? How will you handle it? Do you have the relationships necessary to implement these ideas well? If not, take a step back and build the foundation of trust and understanding you need to change your marketing communications for the better.

CHAPTER 13

Getting Started With Your New Role

Congratulations! You made it to the end of the book. We now crown you the Celestial Monarch of Attention at your organization. You have done a lot of hard work, and you deserve it.

Here's the thing … This book is not written in the order it is meant to be used. In our combined more than 20 years of marketing communications, the most common mistake we see is that most people don't know their targeted audience. From massive, global companies to small businesses to nonprofit organizations that have been around for more than 100 years, all of them have a common problem. They do not know the people that will be responsible for their success. It holds them back in more ways than they could ever imagine. They never gain alignment, they find it impossible to prioritize, and they cannot understand success even when they have it. It needs to "trickle down" (and up) over time.

We recommend you and your team start with *Chapter 2: The Six Audiences Who Matter*. Do the persona exercises outlined in that chapter. Do the research. Conduct surveys. Review the data you have. Talk with people who are and know the most important people. Right now! Stop reading and pull up your calendar. Schedule a three hour session to start doing this work. Include the people who know the audiences best. If no one knows them well, assign someone from the team to start doing the research. If you do not have anyone on the team who can do this work, hire a consultant. If you do not feel able to facilitate the persona conversation, hire someone who can. Stop reading again and schedule another persona meeting for 14 months from now. You will have to do the exercise again, and you might as well get ahead of it this time.

Once you know your audiences, go to *Chapter 9: Measuring Success* and start building your scorecard. Know your benchmarks inside and out so that you can inform future marketing plans and campaigns when the time is right. Ensure that the metrics on your first scorecard are measuring the types of attention the company is receiving. Are you getting awareness (impressions), connected attention (followers/subscribers/web traffic), engaged attention (comments/opens/event interactions), converted attention (marketing qualified leads/applicants), advocate attention (testimonials/case studies)? Also include some benchmarks compared to your competitors.

Once you have audiences and a marketing scorecard, you can start to engage others in the organization. Go to *Chapter 7: Getting Alignment*, and complete the exercises there. Try to really understand the business and what the different leaders on the team are trying to achieve. Ensure you are refocusing these conversations on the targeted audiences. Start asking questions about whether the other leaders think enough of the right people know about the company, its products, or its services. Listen for phrases like "not enough people know about us" or "they would give us a testimonial." Referring to these comments when you finally do introduce the "Five Types of Attention" will help you ground that conversation in something they already understand.

Chapter 8: Making a Plan will follow Chapter 7 naturally in this book. Go through the process with a focus on *Chapter 4: The Five Types of Compelling Content and Chapter 6: The Power of Surround Sound*. Revisit *Chapter 3: Messaging at the Core* as you are working on your plan, but do not let perfect messaging get in the way of creating and beginning to execute your marketing plan. This first year will be all about testing and learning. We have personally seen way too many organizations put off implementing a perfectly good marketing plan because they cannot agree on the specific wording of a positioning statement. The wording of all the messaging will change as you get to learn more about your audiences and try things with them.

When you choose to work on *Chapter 10: Building a Marketing Team* is up to you. If you are severely under-resourced and cannot even begin to implement any parts of the plan, move it up in your process. If you think you can get most of it done with the team you have, whether full-time employees or agency partners, wait to work on this chapter until you are ready to "level up" your marketing and increase your investment in it.

So when do you get to start talking about and working on the "Five Types of Attention?" For most companies, the second year of implementing these ideas is best. They begin to start using some of the language sooner, but they do not center all marketing on it until they know a lot about their audiences and have clarity about the types of attention that are really going to move the needle for them. In year three, they begin to start using the ideas in *Chapter 5: The Four Ways to Bridge Your Content* as they become more sophisticated in their marketing approach.

The good news is that all these chapters are available to you at all times, along with videos, blogs, and eBooks available online.

Glossary

1. **Direct Message (DM)**—A direct message on social media is a private message sent directly to a user's inbox. DMs exist in contrast to public forms of interaction on social media like commenting on an image or posting on a user's timeline.

2. **Engagement Rate**—A social media metric that tells you how much a post is motivating people to interact with it. It's defined as (number of people who engaged with your post divided by the number of people who saw your post) × 100 percent. Typically, a higher engagement rate means your post was more compelling (or at least more likely to provoke a response). Engagement rate is difficult to compare across social networks, as what counts as an "engagement" and what counts as "seeing your post" is different on each network. "Seeing your post" could refer to reach or impressions, while "engagements" may include likes, comments, shares, reactions, and more.

3. **Evergreen Content**—In content marketing, evergreen content is content that ages well and maintains its value over time. Evergreen content is ideal for recycling and repurposing on social media since it does not lose relevance based on the date it's posted. For example, an article on the challenges of being a social media marketer is more likely to be evergreen than an article about TikTok's latest feature update.

4. **Feed**—A feed on social media is a generic term for the stream of content you see from other users. On most social networks, the feed functions as a homepage and is the most common way to see people's posts and engage with them.

5. **Follower**—A follower is a user on social media who has subscribed to see your posts in their feed. Both personal and business accounts can have followers. Your number of followers, or follower count, is a key metric for seeing how your audience on social media is growing or shrinking over time.

6. **Frequency**—A Facebook/Instagram advertising term that refers to how many times your ad was shown to the average user in your target audience. It's calculated by dividing total ad impressions by total ad reach. Frequency over 1.00 means at least some users saw your ad multiple times. This may be positive if your goal is to raise brand awareness and ad recall, but if your frequency is very high you may be wasting your budget and advertising too many times to each user, risking audience ad fatigue.

7. **Impressions**—A social media metric that measures how many times your post has been shown in users' feeds. Unlike with reach, you may count multiple impressions for a single user if they have looked at your post more than once. Each social network counts impressions differently.

8. **Key Performance Indicator (KPI)**—A metric you use to measure your progress toward business goals. In social media marketing, KPIs are the most important stats to track in order to see if you're meeting the objectives of your social strategy. For example, if your primary objective on social was to raise brand awareness, post reach or ad recall lift might be your KPIs.

9. **Listicle**—A list-based article. This type of content is often popular on social media because of its quick, easy-to-digest format. For example, an article like "21 Tips to Massively Increase Instagram Engagement" would be considered a listicle because of its point-by-point breakdown.

10. **Meme**—While the term "meme" (rhymes with "team") originally meant any idea that spread, multiplied, and changed in a viral way, it means something more specific in a social media context. Memes on social media are funny pieces of text, videos, or images that go viral and let users get in on the joke by creating their own variations and sharing them.

11. **Newsjacking**—The technique of hopping on current events with your social media content. Social media managers often engage in newsjacking to seem timely and relevant while gaining exposure by tying their content to key hashtags and conversations around the latest news.

12. **Platform**—The term social media platform is often used to mean the same thing as "social media network" or "social media channel."

However, a social media platform is technically the software behind a social network, including its Application Programming Interface (API), backend, and markup language. The phrase "social media management (SMM) platform," meanwhile, refers to a set of software tools that help SMMs organize their social media accounts.

13. **Reach**—A social media metric that tells you how many people have seen your post. It differs from impressions in that even if a user sees your post multiple times, they still only count as one person reached. Reach is an important metric for understanding how large the audience for your content is and measuring your progress toward spreading brand awareness.

14. **Retargeting**—In social media advertising, retargeting is the technique of targeting ads at users who have interacted with your page or website before. A social media marketer may retarget a user who clicked a Facebook ad for new boots, went to the checkout page, and then didn't complete the sale, for example. Retargeting can be done by either tracking user activities with the Facebook Pixel or uploading a list of past or potential customers to target.

15. **Social Listening**—Social listening is how social media managers track conversations around key topics, terms, brands and more, often with a specialized software tool. Social listening software gathers mentions, comments, hashtags, and relevant posts from across social media to provide insights on what users are talking about and how. Brands often use these insights to tap into key trends and see what people are saying about them and their competitors.

16. **User-Generated Content (UGC)**—Fan-created content promoting a brand. UGC can come in the form of videos, images, posts, audio, reviews, articles, and more. Brands often rely on UGC to get users engaged with their social media campaigns and build trust and loyalty with their followers.

17. **Vanity Metric**—A vanity metric on social media is a statistic that may look like a positive indicator of performance but doesn't actually provide you with valuable insights. Impressions are a classic example as they are often larger than reach, but only tell you how many times people scrolled past a post in their feed without revealing the bigger picture of how popular or engaging the post was.

18. **Viral**—Viral is a term describing content that spreads exponentially on social media. This typically occurs because an increasing number of people share the content with their followers, then their followers share the same content to their followers and so on, creating a snowball effect. Creating content that goes viral is the holy grail of social media marketing, as it means you get a huge audience without spending a cent (Gollin 2020).

References

Casse, P. 1979. *Training for the Cross-Cultural Mind*. Washington, DC: SIETAR International.

Collins, J. 2001. *Good to Great: Why Some Companies Make the Leap and Others Don't*. New York, NY: Harper Business.

Cutlip, S.M. 2013. *The Unseen Power: Public Relations: A History*. New York, NY: Routledge Taylor & Francis Group.

Deutsch, L. May 28, 2014. "13 of Maya Angelou's Best Quotes." *USA Today Network*. www.usatoday.com/story/news/nation-now/2014/05/28/maya-angelou-quotes/9663257/.

Deza, M., and E. Deza. 2009. *Encyclopedia of Distances*, 3rd ed. New York, NY: Springer Publishing.

Gollin, M. January 10, 2020. "The 65 Social Media Terms & Definitions to Know in 2021." *Falcon.io*. www.falcon.io/insights-hub/topics/social-media-management/social-media-terms-buzzwords-definitions-marketers-need-to-know/.

Gaurav, J. 2016. "MECE Framework: Mutually Exclusive, Collectively Exhaustive, and Incredibly Effective." *Humans of Data*, January 28, 2016. https://humansofdata.atlan.com/2016/01/mece-framework-mutually-exclusive/ https://humansofdata.atlan.com/2016/01/mece-framework-mutually-exclusive/.

LinkedIn Talent Solutions. 2015. "The Ultimate List of Hiring Statistics for Hiring Managers, HR Professionals, and Recruiters." *Global Talent Trends*. https://business.linkedin.com/content/dam/business/talent-solutions/global/en_us/c/pdfs/Ultimate-List-of-Hiring-Stats-v02.04.pdf.

Magretta, J. 2011. *Understanding Michael Porter*. Brighton, Massachusetts: Harvard Business Review Press.

National Customer Service Association. n.d. "Using Your Emotional Intelligence to Improve Customer Service." www.nationalcsa.com/articles/emotional-intelligence.php (accessed February 24, 2020).

Nguyen, J., and K. Hallett. May 23, 2021. "How to Use The Emotion Wheel To Better Understand Your Feelings." *MBG Mindfulness*. www.mindbodygreen.com/articles/emotion-wheel.

Obama, B. 2020. *A Promised Land*. Harlow, England: Penguin Books.

Raymond, M. n.d. "Rise in Webinar Hosting During COVID–19." *GoodFirms*. www.goodfirms.co/resources/webinars-during-covid-19 (accessed February 24, 2020).

Revolutionary War and Beyond. n.d. "Benjamin Franklin Letter to Peter Collinson–July 29, 1750." www.revolutionary-war-and-beyond.com/benjamin-franklin-letter-to-peter-collinson-july-29-1750-2.html (accessed April 01, 2021).

Schneider, J. November 06, 2020. "Camera Sales in 2020 Have Plummeted As Much As 54%." *PetaPixel.* https://petapixel.com/2020/11/06/camera-sales-in-2020-have-plummeted-as-much-as-54/.

Snyder, K., and P. Hilal. March 2015. "The Changing Face of B2B Marketing." *Think With Google.* www.thinkwithgoogle.com/consumer-insights/consumer-trends/the-changing-face-b2b-marketing/.

Strong, E.K. Jr. 1925. *The Psychology of Selling and Advertising.* New York, NY: McGraw-Hill Book Company, Inc.

Swift, T. 2014. "Shake It Off." *Big Machine Records.* https://spotify.com/album/2Z51EnLF4Nps4LmulSQPnn (accessed September 14, 2021).

Wikipedia Contributors. n.d. "Public relations." *Wikipedia, The Free Encyclopedia.* Last modified March 22, 2022. https://en.wikipedia.org/wiki/Public_relations.

Zhorob, Dave. 2021. "Podcasts Power Through the Pandemic." *Chartable,* February, 2021. https://chartable.com/blog/2020-year-in-review.

Resources

Slice Communications, LLC

Slice Communications, LLC exists to get people to pay attention to our clients. As a leading Philadelphia marketing and communications agency, it is who we are as people, what gets us up in the morning, and what keeps us going. Since our founding, we have put our collective innate need for attention to work for our clients. We are proud that we have helped them achieve their business goals and grow strategically. Visit us at www.slicecommunications.com to find out the ways in which we can help you achieve your marketing and communications goals.

Additional Publications

Additional publications by Cass Bailey and Dana Schmidt include:

- *How to Create and Promote Thought Leadership Content Every Week*;
- *Employer Brand Communications*;
- *Marketing Planning Simplified*;
- *Engagement Marketing*;
- *An Executive's Guide to Confidence in Marketing*; and
- *Seven Ways PR Can Grow Your Business.*

Check out all of these publications and more at slicecommunications .com/our-publications.

Social Media Day PHL

Cass and Dana are both proud Board Directors of Social Media Day PHL. An official 501(c)(3) nonprofit since 2020, Social Media Day PHL provides professional development and networking experiences to members of the social media, marketing, and communications community. In addition, SMD also hosts an annual #SMDayPHL conference which is the most prominent gathering of communications professionals in the Philadelphia area to hear from the top industry experts. Learn more at smdayphl.com

About the Authors

Cassandra M. Bailey is the CEO of Slice Communications, founder and current Chairwoman of Social Media Day Inc., creator of the "My Mom Is…" children's book series, and has been working in marketing communications for more than 20 years. She believes that integrated public relations, social media, and e-mail marketing efforts are critical for growing businesses and nonprofits looking to accomplish their goals.

With a background in international politics, economics, and philosophy, communications has become her passion, and she has been tapped by various industry associations and the media to share her insights and experiences. She has appeared on *Good Morning America*, *CBS This Morning*, and *The Today Show* and has written for, or been quoted in, *Forbes*, *Philadelphia Magazine*, *Black Enterprise Magazine*, *TheNextWeb*, and a number of other publications. Cass has also been named as a "Rising Star" by the *Women's Business Enterprise National Council* (WBENC) and received the "Brava" award from Philadelphia SmartCEO.

Cass is deeply involved with her community and has served on boards for the Entrepreneurs' Organization of Philadelphia; Business Leadership Forum at The Union League of Philadelphia; Small Business Board at the Greater Philadelphia Chamber of Commerce; Tree House Books; Pennsylvania 30 Day Fund; and Hopeworks. Cass graduated from The Catholic University of America with a degree in international politics, economics, and philosophy. Additionally, she has completed programs in business education from the Goldman Sachs *10,000 Small Businesses Program* and "WBENC Executive Program" at the Tuck School of Business.

Dana M. Schmidt is the Chief Strategy Officer at Slice Communications. Driven by her passion for digital marketing, Dana champions brand storytelling across social media, PR, and e-mail platforms.

Dana's work has taken her from her hometown in Bucks County to New York City, to Denver, and back to Philadelphia—and even earned her an Emmy award along the way for her work on the "Women and

Girls Lead" series at Rocky Mountain PBS. She has shared her expertise with digital marketers through outlets like *Adweek*, *NBC10*, 6ABC's *Inside Story*, and as a speaker at several national conferences, such as *Social Media Day PHL*. Prior to joining Slice Communications, Dana worked in digital marketing at Philadelphia's premier public broadcasting station, WHYY, as well as the city's tourism agency, Visit Philly.

Having earned her Bachelor's degree in Communications from New York University, Dana returned to NYU for her Master of Fine Arts in Creative Writing. Although she'd like to start her novel in her free time, she is more likely out hiking with her husband, Jesse, their son, Cooper, daughter, Mia, and their fluffy husky, Ghost.

Index

CPSIA information can be obtained
at www.ICGtesting.com
Printed in the USA
BVHW091001110722
641515BV00005B/14